Airless Worlds and the Restoration of Psychic Breathing

This book focuses on the recognition and psychoanalytic treatment of a debilitating form of early relational trauma poignantly described by Steven Stern as *airless world syndrome*.

A patient can be said to be *living in an airless world* when one or both parents have failed to recognize, or worse, actively negated their child's subjective experience and needs, instead imposing their subjective reality on the child such that the child had no choice but to adopt the parents' reality as their own. When a child's mind is captured in this way—what Stern calls *identification with negation*—the result is an unconscious bondage to the internalized negating other which can be disabling to the senses of self, personal agency, and realness. With extended clinical examples in every chapter, Stern brings the reader into the depths of each patient's airless world and the co-created *needed relationship* that ultimately, fitfully transforms it.

Written in a detailed yet accessible style, this book is invaluable to psychoanalysts and psychotherapists in practice and in training.

Steven Stern, Psy.D., is Clinical Associate Professor of Psychiatry, Tufts University School of Medicine, and Training and Supervising Analyst at the Massachusetts Institute for Psychoanalysis and The Institute for the Psychoanalytic Study of Subjectivity (NYC). He practices in Portland, ME.

PSYCHOANALYSIS IN A NEW KEY BOOK SERIES
DONNEL STERN
Series Editor

When music is played in a new key, the melody does not change, but the notes that make up the composition do: change in the context of continuity, continuity that perseveres through change. Psychoanalysis in a New Key publishes books that share the aims psychoanalysts have always had, but that approach them differently. The books in the series are not expected to advance any particular theoretical agenda, although to this date most have been written by analysts from the Interpersonal and Relational orientations.

The most important contribution of a psychoanalytic book is the communication of something that nudges the reader's grasp of clinical theory and practice in an unexpected direction. Psychoanalysis in a New Key creates a deliberate focus on innovative and unsettling clinical thinking. Because that kind of thinking is encouraged by exploration of the sometimes surprising contributions to psychoanalysis of ideas and findings from other fields, Psychoanalysis in a New Key particularly encourages interdisciplinary studies. Books in the series have married psychoanalysis with dissociation, trauma theory, sociology, and criminology. The series is open to the consideration of studies examining the relationship between psychoanalysis and any other field—for instance, biology, literary and art criticism, philosophy, systems theory, anthropology, and political theory.

But innovation also takes place within the boundaries of psychoanalysis, and Psychoanalysis in a New Key therefore also presents work that reformulates thought and practice without leaving the precincts of the field. Books in the series focus, for example, on the significance of personal values in psychoanalytic practice, on the complex interrelationship between the analyst's clinical work and personal life, on the consequences for the clinical situation when patient and analyst are from different cultures, and on the need for psychoanalysts to accept the degree to which they knowingly satisfy their own wishes during treatment hours, often to the patient's detriment.

A full list of all titles in this series is available at:
https://www.routledge.com/Psychoanalysis-in-a-New-Key-Book-Series/book-series/LEAPNKBS

Airless Worlds and the Restoration of Psychic Breathing

Working Psychoanalytically with Early Relational Trauma

Steven Stern

Routledge
Taylor & Francis Group

LONDON AND NEW YORK

Designed cover image: © Edward A. Mason (1919–2007)

First published 2026
by Routledge
4 Park Square, Milton Park, Abingdon, Oxon OX14 4RN

and by Routledge
605 Third Avenue, New York, NY 10158

Routledge is an imprint of the Taylor & Francis Group, an informa business

British Library Cataloguing-in-Publication Data
A catalogue record for this book is available from the British Library

ISBN: 978-1-032-95507-0 (hbk)
ISBN: 978-1-032-95290-1 (pbk)
ISBN: 978-1-003-58523-7 (ebk)

DOI: 10.4324/9781003585237

Typeset in Times New Roman
by Deanta Global Publishing Services, Chennai, India

For Laura, whose love, astute feedback, and tolerance for the time-consuming nature of my work constituted the "air" within which this book came to life.

Contents

Preface

Elizabeth Corpt

In the summer of 2023, as I was writing my keynote address for the International Association for Psychoanalytic Self Psychology (IAPSP)'s upcoming fall meetings in Chicago, Steven Stern's concept of airless worlds suddenly leapt to the forefront of my mind, causing me to gasp. A gasp: that instinctive and sudden taking in of an extra bit of air in response to a jarring and breathtaking thought. Let me explain. At the time, I was writing about Heinz Kohut and his relationship to his Jewishness and to the unfolding horror of the Nazis in Europe. More specifically, I was addressing Kohut's dissociative erasure of the cascade of losses that befell him and his extended family in Vienna, and his absolute need to flee Austria to save his own physical and psychic life. In my effort to empathically grasp the extent of Kohut's experience, I became deeply absorbed in the words and profound sense of loss communicated by Kohut's son, Thomas, who lamented never having been able to know this painful and understandably dissociated part of his father's life, and the inevitable impact this had on his father's work. My association to Nazism and the barbaric cruelty of their project was condensed into a vision of the gas chambers and the calculated intention of the Nazis to relegate all Jews, homosexuals, and all others deemed unacceptable, to airless worlds: worlds of certain death. Hence my gasp as I suddenly made the connection, in my mind, between the airless worlds of the gas chambers that haunted Kohut and his work, and Stern's compelling concept of airless worlds.

Stern's clinical concept of "airless worlds" was already one that I, and numerous others, had found particularly compelling and useful in the consulting room, but, in that moment, the "world" to which this concept referred suddenly took on an added dimension, beyond that of the consulting room to the wider world of the social/cultural/political context. It seemed to me as though Stern was excavating and reworking a crucial and missing piece of the origins of Self Psychology, and by doing so, was providing a much needed understanding of some of the darker aspects of human nature and their complex emotional sequelae. In response to my keynote remarks, Steve asked whether I'd be willing to write the preface to his new book.

Before I expand on these thoughts, I'd like to say a few more words about why I think Stern's metaphors of airless worlds and breathing together have so captured us. These evocative metaphors about breathing speak to something basic, universal, and fundamental about life. Concretely speaking, we know there can be no such thing as actual physical survival in a completely airless world. Stern, however, is after something far deeper and more complex here: something about the link between breathing, feeling, and being. Stern links breathing and feeling to the recognition and meaning-making processes of early life, and thus to the very forming of subjectivity. He asks us to consider the intersubjective contexts that can expand or constrict a life. Breathing and feeling are of particular interest to those of us who are drawn to understanding the origins of psychic suffering, meaning making, and the intricacies of therapeutic care and cure. With seeming effortlessness, Stern considers the contributions of a variety of psychoanalytic thinkers as he works to delineate his own unique psychoanalytic contribution.

As I am writing this, we are living through the recent tragic loss of my dear friend and our dear colleague, Donna Orange. Donna, who was invited to write the preface to Steven Stern's last book, *Needed Relationships and Psychoanalytic Healing*, found Stern's ideas of needed relationships and relational fittedness an elegant and thoughtful contribution to contemporary psychoanalysis. I wholeheartedly agree with Donna's assessment, and it is my honor to have been invited to follow in her footsteps in writing this preface. Although Donna has now ceased to physically breathe, or to offer us the opportunity to breathe along with her, she still provides us psychic oxygen. This is the very relational complexity Stern is addressing: how certain relational contexts have the capacity to empower and strengthen us, or diminish, and even extinguish us. How human beings are with each other matters greatly and can make all the difference.

Building from and extending Kohut's use of the metaphor of oxygen needed throughout the lifespan, Stern lays out the fullness of his concept of airless world syndrome as an extension of and complement to his concept of needed relationships. Here, he highlights the importance of and speaks to what he sees as the under-theorized complexities of "identification with parental negation" and the significant role it plays in cementing "psychic captivities," and foiling needed therapeutic relationships. As his rich clinical stories confirm, it is not only dissociation and splitting that result from early trauma, but also bondage to negation within early needed relationships which make for the complex and intricate work required in dedicated therapeutic relationships. Stern offers a master class in navigating through subtle shifts in feeling states and the intricacy of protective retreats. He understands that patients' sensitivities to any misreading or premature understanding of their experience can trigger re-traumatization. These experience-near metaphors of airless worlds and psychic breathing, synthesized from his patients' expressed descriptions of suffering—bondage, toxicity, suffocation, neglect, colonization, erasure, and the like—allow him to tailor his fittedness ever more thoughtfully. His concepts of deconstruction, re-subjectification, breathing together, and complex selfobject connection further complete this framework: an invaluable clinical and theoretical perspective deeply respectful of individuality, dignity, and the complexity of therapeutic change.

Stern's metaphors of psychic death or near-death experiences that accompany profound and sustained erasures and negations of emotional needs and subjectivity are also applicable to understanding the stifling, suffocation, or erasure of a people, or of a kind of people, or a way of being, or living, in the larger world. We need look no further than the final words of George Floyd's now iconic plea of "I can't breathe" to see the connection. Floyd's final words inspired an outpouring of empathic resonance and support from those who could relate to and/or empathize with others who suffer the constancy of constricted breathing, continual suffocation, or unbearable bouts of air hunger, while living in a society that refuses to grant them the fullness of their humanity.

As I read through Steven Stern cases and followed the elegance of his thinking and considered the delicacy, stamina, and dedication required to do this clinical work, I found myself curious about the larger contexts out of which these unique airless worlds emerged and proliferated. How would we begin to think about healing from societal negation? How do we provide the needed relational and societal contexts out of which healthy humans can grow? What causes human beings to suffocate one another, or the planet as a whole? Although these questions lie beyond the scope of this book, Stern's ideas are immensely useful in providing us a new language from which to consider intimate and complex issues of justice, fairness, dignity, and respect for all beings, from the moment of birth onwards, both within and outside the consulting room.

Acknowledgements

My first acknowledgement goes to my patients, past and present. They have been the true collaborators in my career-long effort both to understand what our patients in general most need from us and to co-create healing relationships, which are unique with each patient but are informed by the cumulative wisdom accrued from my relationships with all of them.

It takes a village for any individual to do creative work. My village consists of the many friends and colleagues who have encouraged and supported my writing over the years. The following group have been especially supportive: James Anderson, Jessica Butzel, William Coburn, Elizabeth Corpt, Heather Ferguson, Robert Galatzer-Levy, Jane Jordan, Peter Kaufman, Ruth Kavesh, Sarah Mendelsohn, William Redd, William Reich, Peter Rudnytsky, Estelle Shane, Joyce Slochower, Donnel Stern, Jeffrey Stern, Shaké Topalian, Mark Trewartha, Joye Weisel-Barth, Peter Wilk, the late Lewis Aron, and the late Donna Orange.

As was the case for my first book, the cover art for this book is an enhanced-image photograph by Edward A. Mason (1919–2007), my first professional mentor and life-long friend. As with my first book, Ed's daughter, Andrea Nolin, applied her own artistic gifts and digital skills in helping select the photographic image and creating a preliminary cover design incorporating that image. I also thank Ed's widow, Jean Mason (who recently celebrated her hundredth birthday) for her support over the years and her permission to use Ed's photographs.

All of the brief case examples in the Introduction—Mary, Tom, Clint, Lisa, and Kara—I have written about at greater length in previous publications. These include: "The Self as a Relational Structure," *Psychoanalytic Dialogues*, *12*: 693–714 (2002); "Identification, Repetition and Psychological Growth," *Psychoanalytic Psychology*, *19*: 722–738

(2002); "The Conundrum of Self-Care," *Contemporary Psychoanalysis, 43*: 605–620 (2007); and *Needed Relationships and Psychoanalytic Healing*. Routledge, 2017.

The case of Clint in Chapter 2 and Part 1 of the case of Philip in Chapter 3 are based on sections from Stern, S. (2024), "Breathing Together: Needed Relationships and Complex Selfobjects," *Psychoanalysis, Self and Context, 19*: 274–285.

Chapter 1 is based on: Stern, S. (2019), "Airless Worlds: The Traumatic Sequelae of Identification with Parental Negation," *Psychoanalytic Dialogues, 29*: 435–450.

Chapter 4 is based on: Stern, S. (2023), "Airless Worlds and Couples Therapy," *Psychoanalysis, Self and Context*: 164–179.

Chapter 5 is based on: Stern, S. (2021), "Analtyic Adoption of the Psychically Homeless," *Psychoanalysis, Self and Context, 16*: 24–42.

Large portions of the Appendix derive from two earlier publications: (1) Stern, S. (2002a), "The Self as a Relational Structure," *Psychoanalytic Dialogues, 12*: 693–714; and (2) Stern, S. (2002b), "Identification, Repetition and Psychological Growth," *Psychoanalytic Psychology, 19*: 722–738.

When I look I am seen, so I exist.

(**D.W. Winnicott**, 1971, p. 114)

Introduction

When I first met Mary[1] she was an emaciated waif—a 50-year-old chronic anorexic who was clearly very bright and self-aware but so anxious, tentative, and lacking in vibrancy that I knew right away I was encountering someone who had been terribly damaged. Though not in denial about her eating disorder, Mary proceeded initially as if this were not a major concern. Her chief concern was that her two previous lengthy therapies had not helped her deal with her paralyzing self-criticalness—the legacy of her relationship with her toxically controlling and critical mother. The mother, who seemed primitively organized, had treated Mary as a defective object whom she needed to monitor and control. This included monitoring and regulating her eating and bowel functions—the latter through administering frequent, medically unnecessary enemas. Mary had had to read her mother's mind and moods and accommodate to her needs or face her angry, disapproving, guilt-inducing withdrawal. The result, Mary was aware, was that she had internalized her mother's harshly critical, totalizing voice. Toward the end of that first session I made a simple, expressive interpretation: "Your mother is *on* you!" Her silent, flowing tears registered the deep recognition I knew she was feeling.

I could make such a confident interpretation because it quickly became painfully clear that Mary suffered from an extreme form of a particular kind of psychic damage that I had been studying for some time. I had noticed it first in one of my control cases when I was an analytic candidate. Tom was a stronger person than Mary. Yet, despite his privileged background and elite education, he felt paralyzed in his capacity to move forward in his life, personally and professionally. Like Mary, he had a parent who had superimposed her needs and psychic realities on him, failing to recognize and support his needs and right to his own developmental process and path.

DOI: 10.4324/9781003585237-1

And like Mary, he did not really know his own mind, including his feelings and needs. Thus, long into young-adult life, he organized himself, part-consciously and part-unconsciously, around trying to be the kind of person his mother perceived him to be and needed him to be. It was as if, in major areas of functioning, both Mary and Tom continued to be controlled by the mind of another, not really knowing or understanding that a certain kind of usurpation or colonization had taken place.

I am not implicating mothers as the villains of the piece. The same kind of dynamic I am describing between a mother and child can also occur between a father and child. Clint, a patient in his 60s, had been terrorized and ruthlessly devalued by a tyrannical, sadistic father throughout his adolescence and young adulthood. Several years into therapy he revealed that throughout his adult life he had had the recurring nightmare that he was trapped underground beneath a sealed manhole. He could see light coming down around the edges, but there was no possibility of escape. It was only with therapy that this image took on meaning as representing his fully sealed off subjective self, which had been assaulted, strangulated, and imprisoned since childhood.

I call the common features shared by this group of patients *airless world syndrome*. A patient can be said to be living in an airless world when one or both parents have failed to recognize and/or have actively negated their child's subjective reality and needs. Instead they have imposed *their* subjective reality (including their subjective experience of that child) on the child such that they had no choice but to adopt the parent's reality as their own. When such mental occupation occurs early enough, a child may never have experienced themselves as having any independent subjective self apart from what has been un-empathically reflected back to them by their parents. Consequently, even after the child has grown up and physically separated from their family of origin, the mental suffocation that characterized their early *relational environment* may still, to a significant degree, define their *internal mental environment*; though this internal state of affairs is occurring largely outside of conscious awareness.

After working with a series of patients struggling with some form of this syndrome, I came to see a lawfulness in the complex dynamic underpinnings of their subjective worlds and objective disabilities. When a patient's subjective experience and self have never been accurately or empathically perceived and responded to by reality-defining parental others, but rather have been distorted, often in highly pejorative, damaging ways, the result is a disabling deformation in the senses of self and personal agency that I do not find fully captured in other closely related theoretical/developmental accounts such as Winnicott's (1960) false self, Kohut's (1971, 1977, 1984) narcissistically compromised self, Brandchaft's (1994, 2010) structures of pathological accommodation, and the dissociated self-states of contemporary relational theory (e.g., Bromberg, 1998, 2011). What's missing in these seminal theories is a full appreciation of the identificatory elements in the patient's psychological organization and ways of functioning. These elements *were* recognized by Ferenczi (1933) in his initial illumination of the phenomenon of "identification with the aggressor" as a disabling consequence of childhood sexual trauma. But with few exceptions (e.g., Frankel, 2002; Howell, 2014; Stern, 2002a, 2002b, 2019), his ideas about identification have not been fully brought forward and recontextualized within a contemporary relational-intersubjective-developmental framework. Two further examples highlight the identificatory dynamic at the core of this syndrome.

Lisa and Kara

Lisa, a remarkably resilient, professionally successful woman in her 30s, had, as an adolescent and young adult, taken on the role of the selfless, responsible daughter, focusing on everyone else's welfare—a role her family members seemed all too happy to have her play. Indeed, whenever she protested or demanded something for herself, she was told by her mother that she was selfish and irresponsible. Now, as an adult, she would host holiday dinners, mediate family disputes, bail her two low-life brothers out of financial and legal scrapes, and generally be on call, especially to her mother, whose relationship to Lisa still consisted of asking Lisa to do things for her and making her feel guilty when she refused.

Over the first year of treatment, Lisa got more and more in touch with her resentment about this state of affairs and became determined to make a change in her responses. The problem was that whenever she contemplated acting on her resentment, say by refusing to do something she considered inappropriate or unreasonable, she would immediately feel intensely guilty, accusing herself of being selfish, irresponsible, and negative, exactly in the style of her mother. At the outset of treatment this latter voice was by far the louder and more compelling: Lisa was mostly the compliant caretaker with occasional eruptions of anger in other safer arenas such as work (where her professional status protected her).

Kara, a married 30-year-old woman, was highly competent though insecure in her job as a human resources director of a growing software company. Early in treatment she spent many sessions talking about interactions with her husband that left her in states of emotional fragmentation. Over time, I came to discern a pattern to these interactions. Kara would present herself to her husband as overwhelmed by the routine problems in her life: problems at work, problems of time management and organization, and problems in her outside relationships. Jim, a devotee of self-improvement programs of all kinds, whose hyper-organized, controlling style was the opposite of Kara's more intuitive approach, would seize upon these requests as opportunities not only to help Kara with the problem at hand, for which he always had a competent solution, but also as invitations to help Kara reform her supposedly undisciplined, disorganized ways. Kara would then have a telling response to Jim's interventions: She would take in all of his advice as if it were the gospel which she both believed and felt she needed to hear in order to keep her own self-improvement efforts on track; at the same time, she would feel inexplicably worse about herself and angry with Jim, often failing to implement his suggestions.

How to understand Kara's particular form of identificatory bondage? I learned that her father, an alcoholic, sociopathic, white-collar criminal, tended to be critical of Kara when he was available at all. He became a traumatically de-idealized figure, not to mention completely unavailable, when he went to prison for the first time during her adolescence. Understandably, Kara found in Jim a scrupulously honest, strong-willed, very attentive (selfobject) husband whom she could idealize, entrust herself to, and seek guidance from in a way she never could with her father. Unfortunately, because of Jim's limited empathic capacities and a tendency to be overly controlling and critical, Kara received a toxic mixture of some responses she needed and some she decidedly did not. (See also Eigen's [1999] concept of "toxic nourishment.") Yet, she still identified with Jim's responses, and these identifications exerted a fragmenting effect on her momentary feeling about herself and sense of self.

Although quite different in many ways, Lisa and Kara shared a mostly unconscious identificatory bond with a primary needed other (Lisa's mother; Kara's husband), grounded in traumatic family histories of a particular kind.

Namely, their subjectivities and certain core developmental needs had been systematically neglected and/or negated, thereby weakening their senses of self and personal agency, and leaving them reliant on (and identified with) the minds of their negating significant others.

When a child's psychic reality and needs have not been sufficiently recognized or developmentally supported, or worse, have been actively negated by early caregivers, the result is a form of identificatory bondage wherein the child's (later, adult patient's) primary way of functioning in certain areas is through identification with the other's perspective, judgments, and requirements. In effect, the child-now-adult unconsciously cedes to the other the power to define the self, even when the other's construal and treatment of the patient is highly toxic (again, see Eigen, 1999). The adult patient trapped in such an airless intrapsychic world knows at some level that they are trapped, and desperately wants to be liberated and enabled psychically to breathe. The problem is that, within the logic of the patient's child-self, which is still held captive within the internalized parents' orbit of reality, the only way out is through longed-for parental recognition and affirmation that never came and, most likely, never will come in the future. The analytic therapist hopes to acquire the transferential power to create a breach in this closed airless system of the patient's experience of self as defined by the parents. But the acquisition of such influence is by no means assured, even in treatment relationships that are in many ways positive and therapeutic. This book is intended to help therapists help their patients who are struggling with some form of this syndrome.

General Considerations

Airless world syndrome exists on a continuum of severity, where severity is defined by either the degree of disability in particular areas or the pervasiveness of the total areas of disability affected by the early relational milieu. Factors affecting the severity and pervasiveness of disability include: (1) the age at which parental usurpation began; (2) the totality of parental distortion and/or need for control, which is roughly correlated with the severity (primitiveness) of parental psychopathology; (3) the inadvertent and, especially, any intentional destructiveness inherent in the parents' treatment of the child; (4) whether there was any good-enough, attuned parenting available from either parent; (5) the counteracting influence of siblings, relatives, and other significant figures as the child grew up; and finally (6) the "X-factor"—the seemingly innate/constitutional areas of adaptive strength, resilience, and capacity to resist parental control that a given child brought to the situation of their upbringing.

Many of the psychological elements I am grouping under the rubric of "airless world syndrome" are familiar to analytically informed psychotherapists. And even the combination of these elements, or at least many of them, have much in common with already identified, developmentally based disorders, syndromes, theories, and frames of reference. I have learned much from the psychoanalytic thinkers who have preceded me in writing about related problems and how to treat them. I summarize some of these influences in Chapter 1. But I wouldn't be writing about the topic at such length unless I felt there was something new and useful to say about it. The patients I am grouping under the rubric of airless world syndrome present a particular set of difficulties that, in my experience, can be highly refractory even to sophisticated and contemporary forms of analytic treatment. This is because of the extent to which their minds, senses of self, and ways of treating themselves and others have been "captured" and defined by negating others, such that there is little to no "air" or "space" between their identificatory experience of self and a truer sense of self grounded in their own genuine feelings, needs, rhythms, perceptions (including self-perceptions), interests, desires, judgments, and values. I believe this is a more disabling intrapsychic configuration than has been commonly recognized. It requires a grasp of the nature and power of the psychic forces involved to gain meaningful therapeutic traction and help such patients resume psychic breathing.

Clinical Implications

In my 2019 paper (see Chapter 1) I identified two therapeutic elements or processes I had found to be uniquely relevant with airless world patients: *deconstruction* and *re-subjectification*. Deconstruction refers to the process of trying to help the patient, in direct and indirect ways, loosen the grip of the toxically negating identifications, attitudes, and organizing assumptions that have exerted a strangulating and controlling effect on their subjective reality since childhood. Re-subjectification refers to all the therapeutic processes involved in helping patients learn to recognize, develop, integrate, and use their own authentic feelings, needs, desires, perceptions, interests, and judgments as a resource in navigating the complexities of their lives.

(See also Shaw's [2014] similar ideas about "subjectifying processes" in the analytic treatment of victims of traumatic narcissists; and Pinato, Moia, and Negri's [2012] creative work on "the process of image subjectification.") In this book I develop these ideas further, adding greater specificity to how these processes play out in treatment.

A central dimension of the re-subjectification process, which I alluded to but did not fully develop in the 2019 paper (Chapter 1), is the *selfobject dimension* of the therapeutic relationship (Kohut, 1971, 1977, 1984). Since airless world syndrome is quintessentially a disorder of the sense of self, including the senses of realness and personal agency, treatment requires a developmental process wherein the patient is gradually freed and enabled to more fully "inhabit" themselves—their authentic experience of their own being within their relational worlds. This needed re-subjectification and growth process is greatly facilitated if the patient is able to form a selfobject transference connection with the therapist. Yet, I will argue, the nature of the selfobject connection the adult traumatized patient needs is more complex than the familiar selfobject transference configurations identified by Kohut: mirroring, idealizing, and twinship. In this book (mainly in Chapters 2 and 3), I introduce the idea of a *complex selfobject* experience and demonstrate what this looks like and how it can work in airless world cases.

A complex selfobject connection takes time to develop and is directly related to the idea of progressive relational *fittedness*, a term that comes from Louis Sander's (2008) developmental theory and was central to my understanding of *the needed relationship*, as articulated in my 2017 book, *Needed Relationships and Psychoanalytic Healing*. As patient and therapist get to know each other within their analytic frame, the analyst aims to develop an increasingly complex and holistic grasp of the nature of the patient's struggles and how to *meet* those struggles in ways that begin to make a difference in the patient's ability to understand them and evolve toward greater mastery of them. As the patient comes to experience the analyst as recognizing, and truly helping them with, their struggles in progressively fitted ways, an increasingly complex selfobject connection forms between them—a connection I think of, metaphorically, as *breathing together*. It requires the experience of breathing together to restart *the patient's* capacity for psychic breathing, which had been strangulated throughout their "airless" childhood. It is difficult to fully capture in words what I mean by the phenomenon of breathing together. The way I would put it is: As a complex selfobject connection develops over time in highly nonlinear ways, an *intersubjective pathway* with both conscious and uncon-scious dimensions opens up between patient and analyst, creating a sense of in-sync-ness or connectedness (Geist, 2009) that progressively, albeit fit-fully, deepens and strengthens the relationship, greatly enhancing its trans-formational potential.

These concepts—the complex selfobject and breathing together—go to the crux of a paradox or dialectic that lies at the heart of this book regard-ing the nature of therapeutic action. This book is about airless world phe-nomena and aims to provide an in-depth understanding both of the nature of airless world problems and the specific implications that understand-ing holds for therapeutic intervention. The paradox is that these specific elements of understanding and treating airless world patients cannot sim-ply be applied; they must be emergent within the *total needed relation-ship* that forms over time—that is, a relationship oriented to and shaped by the patient-as-a-whole, not simply their struggles with airless world issues. This paradox relates to my general thinking about therapeutic action in ana-lytic treatment, which has been evolving since writing my book on needed relationships.

The *Needed Relationships* book implicitly posed the meta-theoretical question: *What level of constructs do we need to be using to think com-plexly enough about the problem of how we fit what we do clinically to what each patient needs?* My general answer requires making a distinction between two kinds of psychoanalytic construct—*holistic* and *categorical*. Both Sander's recognition theory and my needed relationships framework are what I think of as holistic models. Holistic concepts stand in contrast to categorical concepts. Concepts like needed relationship, fittedness, meet-ing the patient, specificity of recognition and connection, and breathing together are holistic concepts. They refer to the whole process of two whole persons interacting in ways that will be helpful to one of them in the com-plex wholeness of the present analytic moment. Holistic concepts are ways of imagining the relationship as a whole, whereas categorical concepts identify particular dimensions of both the patient's psychological organiza-tion and the analytic relationship.

Psychoanalysis needs both kinds of construct, but too often in our his-tory theorists have made the error of mistaking the latter for the former—of mistaking the part for the whole (see Stern, 2017, Introduction and Chapter 5). Why does this matter? It matters because when categorical concepts are confused with holistic ones there is a tendency to be looking for that categorical dimension everywhere as opposed to approaching every session without preconception or, as Bion (1970) wrote: "without memory or desire." It also matters because naming the *relationship-as-a-whole* as an overarching construct recognizes the complexity of all that is involved in achieving progressive fittedness with developmentally traumatized patients.

My construct of airless worlds is a categorical concept. It refers to a particular pattern of intrapsychic organization, the understanding of which offers greater traction in working with certain patients. But with any such patient, I am also always trying to bear in mind that their airless world dynamics are only part of their psychological organization and that it is their psychological organization as-a-whole with which I must try to connect and achieve fittedness. Moreover, no two patients' airless worlds are alike. Thus, in applying the model with a given patient it is best to hold the airless world paradigm loosely, or lightly, as Donna Orange (1995, 2011) would say. Held loosely, elements of the model find their way into our work with a given patient but integrated within the superordinate project of achieving progressive fittedness with that patient-as-a-whole over time. It is our ability to hold this holistic/categorical dialectic in mind as an orienting frame that ultimately, over time, enables the experience of progressive fittedness, and hence complex-selfobject connectedness, to emerge in the treatment of airless world problems.

Plan of the Book

This book aims to: (1) flesh out the theory of airless worlds introduced in my 2019 paper; (2) offer in-depth clinical illustrations of both the nature of the problem and the treatment paradigm I have evolved for working analytically with patients suffering from airless world syndrome; (3) extend and further delineate my ideas about *needed analytic relationships* (Stern, 2017); (4) introduce the concepts of a *complex selfobject* and *breathing together*; (5) apply the theory of airless worlds to couples therapy; (6) propose the concept of *analytic adoption* as a way to think about our work with certain patients who grew up in situations of extreme forms of parental negation, neglect, and/or abuse; and, finally, (7) introduce the idea of *management* as a relational tool for those who have grown up in airless family systems and still struggle in their relationships with family-of-origin members.

Chapter 1 is essentially the original 2019 paper from *Psychoanalytic Dialogues*.

Chapters 2 and 3 are the "beating heart" of the book—namely, in-depth accounts of the therapeutic processes involved in working with three patients struggling with airless world problems of various kinds. In these chapters I explicitly link my thinking about needed relationships with my theory of airless worlds and introduce the concepts of a *complex selfobject* connection and *breathing together* as central to the healing process. As noted earlier, in the original 2019 paper I proposed two general categories of intervention specific to patients living in airless intrapsychic worlds: *deconstruction* and *re-subjectification*. In Chapters 2 and 3, these concepts are fleshed out, illustrated, and integrated into my more general thinking about both needed relationships and therapeutic action.

Chapter 4 begins with a proposed expansion of the airless world rubric to include different "varieties of airlessness" not explicitly named in my 2019 paper (Chapter 1). It then goes on to apply airless world theory to work with couples exhibiting airlessness of a certain kind in their relationships—namely, a breakdown in their capacity for dialogue, especially around their most charged issues. Using an in-depth clinical example of a couple whose capacity for useful dialogue around significant issues had broken down over many years, the chapter illustrates how I work with such couples, seeking to "introduce psychic air" into their airless marital systems. The chapter also expands Kohut's thinking about analytic empathy with individuals to include *empathy with the needs of the system.*

Chapter 5 introduces the idea of *analytic adoption* as relevant to relationships that can form over time with a subgroup of patients whose experiences in their families of origin were so traumatically negating, neglectful, and/or abusive that they were essentially emotional orphans. The chapter is organized around my 40-year treatment of a woman who grew up in such an environment and illustrates therapeutic principles that emerged from this work and facilitated a profound degree of healing. Symbolizing the unique nature of our relationship, around our twenty-fifth year I coined the term "thamily" to capture the complex paradoxes embedded in our work together.

In **Chapter 6** I adopt a more pragmatic writing style to address the problem, for patients who have grown up in negating families, of how, as adults, to conduct (really, survive) their relationships with their still-problematic family-of-origin members. These patients are often stuck in frustrating, dysfunctional, and destructive patterns of interaction with their family members. I have found the concept of *management* to be useful in helping them realistically orient to what is possible at this point in their lives with their parents (and sometimes adult siblings). While there are certain skills involved in this kind of relating, effective management usually requires intensive analytic work and the co-creation over time of a needed relationship with the analyst. It is through the emergence of the needed relationship that the patient is enabled to separate psychologically from family-of-origin members and evolve the greater sense of personal agency necessary for the full development and refinement of management skills. I illustrate such a therapeutic process with a patient who had long-standing difficulties with his mother, father, and brother.

Note

1 As noted in the Acknowledgments, all of the brief case examples in this Introduction—Mary, Tom, Clint, Lisa, and Kara—I have written about at greater length in previous publications (Stern, 2002a, 2002b, 2007, 2017). The case descriptions here are partially quoted from those earlier writings. The brief description of Clint's situation with his father anticipates a more extended account of our work in Chapter 2.

References

Bion, W.R. (1970). *Attention and interpretation.* London: Karnac.

Brandchaft, B. (1994). To free the spirit from its cell. In R.D. Stolorow, G.E. Atwood, & B. Brandchaft (Eds.), *The intersubjective perspective* (pp. 57–76). Northvale, NJ: Jason Aronson.

Brandchaft, B. (2010). Toward an emancipatory psychoanalysis. In B. Brandchaft, S. Doctors, & D. Sorter (Eds.), *Toward an emancipatory psychoanalysis: Brandchaft's intersubjective vision* (pp. 9–27). New York, NY and London: Routledge.

Bromberg, P.M. (1998). *Standing in the spaces: Essays on clinical process, trauma, and dissociation.* Hillsdale, NJ: The Analytic Press.

Bromberg, P.M. (2011). *The shadow of the tsunami and the growth of the relational mind.* New York, NY and London: Routledge.

Eigen, M. (1999). *Toxic nourishment.* London: Karnac.

Ferenczi, S. (1933). Confusion of tongues between adults and the child. In M. Balint (Ed.), *Final contributions to the problems and methods of psychoanalysis* (pp. 156–167). London: Karnac.

Frankel, J. (2002). Exploring Ferenczi's concept of identification with the aggressor: Its role in trauma, everyday life, and the therapeutic relationship. *Psychoanalytic Dialogues, 12*: 101–140.

Geist, R.A. (2009). Empathy, connectedness, and the evolution of boundaries in self psychological treatment. *International Journal of Psychoanalytic Self Psychology, 4*: 165–180.

Howell, E. (2014). Ferenczi's concept of identification with the aggressor: Understanding dissociative structure with interacting victim and abuser self-states. *American Journal of Psychoanalysis, 74*: 48–59.

Kohut, H. (1971). *The analysis of the self: A systematic approach to the psychoanalytic treatment of narcissistic personality disorders.* New York, NY: International Universities Press.

Kohut, H. (1977). *The restoration of the self.* New York, NY: International Universities Press.

Kohut, H. (1984). *How does analysis cure?* (A. Goldberg & P. Stepansky, Eds.). Chicago, IL: University of Chicago Press.

Orange, D.M. (1995). *Emotional understanding: Studies in psychoanalytic epistemology.* New York, NY: Guilford.

Orange, D.M. (2011). *The suffering stranger.* New York, NY and London: Routledge.

Pinato, M., Moia, A., & Negri, I. (2012). Figures of understanding: The process of image subjectifcation. *International Journal of Psychoanalytic Self Psychology, 7*: 45–68.

Sander, L. (2008). *Living systems, evolving consciousness, and the emerging person: A selection of papers from the life work of Louis Sander.* (G. Amadei & I. Bianchi, Eds.). New York, NY and London: Routledge.

Shaw, D. (2014). *Traumatic narcissism: Relational systems of subjugation.* New York, NY: Routledge.

Stern, S. (2002a). The self as a relational structure: A dialogue with multiple-self theory. *Psychoanalytic Dialogues, 12*: 693–714.

Stern, S. (2002b), Identification, repetition, and psychological growth: An expansion of relational theory. *Psychoanalytic Psychology, 19*: 722–738.

Stern, S. (2007). The conundrum of self-care. *Contemporary Psychoanalysis, 43*: 605–620.

Stern, S. (2017). *Needed relationships and psychoanalytic healing: A holistic relational perspective on the therapeutic process.* London and New York, NY: Routledge.

Stern, S. (2019). Airless worlds: The traumatic sequelae of identification with parental negation. *Psychoanalytic Dialogues, 29*: 435–450.

Winnicott, D.W. (1960/1965), The theory of the parent-infant relationship. In D.W. Winnicott (Ed.), *The maturational processes and the facilitating environment* (pp. 37–55). New York, NY: International Universities Press.

Winnicott, D.W. (1967/1971). Mirror-role of mother and family in child development. In D.W. Winnicott (Ed.), *Playing and reality* (pp. 111–118). London: Tavistock.

Chapter 1

Airless Worlds

The Traumatic Sequelae of Identification with Parental Negation

Identification and Dissociation: A Complex Interaction

Few relationally oriented psychoanalysts would dispute the importance of identification as a developmental organizer of human subjectivity. Indeed, we take its centrality so for granted that, while explicit reference to its role in our patients' life struggles still weaves in and out of our published clinical narratives, these references are mainly descriptive and in passing rather than being subjected to the bright light reserved for core causal dynamics. Instead, *dissociation* and its sister concept, the multiplicity of self-experience, have captured our post-modern collective imagination as the explanatory constructs that seem most generative in describing both the "normal" organization of the mind and the defensive rigidities that result from our patients' most profound developmental traumas (e.g., Mitchell, 1993; Davies, 1996; Pizer, 1998; D.B. Stern, 2010; Bromberg, 2011; Schore 2011). My aim in this book is to tilt the scale back in the direction of identification, arguing that these two "principles of mental functioning" exist in complex interaction in our patients—an interaction that needs to be reflected in our theories as well.

Both of these dynamic principles (as they relate to early trauma) have their roots in Ferenczi's (1933) seminal paper, "The Confusion of Tongues Between Adults and the Child." In it, he reasserted the reality of childhood sexual trauma and brilliantly described what he found to be the two central and most therapeutically challenging psychological after-effects of such trauma. The first he had discovered from his repeated observation that his patients who had experienced early trauma tended to passively *identify themselves with him* rather than express their own authentic feelings and perceptions. He interpreted this as an involuntary, self-protective response

DOI: 10.4324/9781003585237-2

to being enlisted by the transgressor, first in the traumatic encounters themselves, and later in his ensuing guilty feelings. The second dynamic Ferenczi called "*splitting of the personality*." These patients, he observed, saw things in part as the "innocent children" they had been before the trauma, and in part as the "shocked" person, now having to develop precocious, adult-like modes of functioning to cope with their new relational realities.

In our recent literature, while the vicissitudes of dissociation have been extensively investigated, with few exceptions (e.g., Frankel, 2002; Howell, 2014; Stern 2002a, 2002b, 2019) the same has not been true for identification. Thus, our understanding of its contribution to our patients' struggles is under-developed. This is no small matter because an in-depth exploration of the identificatory elements in the human response to relational trauma generates a different mental model than a theory focusing predominantly on dissociation.

In the latter, the main source of difficulty arises from the rigid dissociation of what Sullivan (1953) called "not me" self-states from those that are both more affectively tolerable and more recognizable and acceptable as "me" (e.g., D.B. Stern, 2010; Bromberg, 2011). The "not me" states are thought to carry the unsymbolized, overwhelming affects associated with the patient's experience of, and response to, the original trauma. The clinical problem is one of facilitating the cognitive-affective ownership of these dissociated states. This occurs through their emergence (via enactments) and articulation within the intersubjective analytic field.

In the identification-based model I have been developing, the central problem is not the dissociation of not-me states, but rather the disabling quality of the patient's *dominant experience of* me—a legacy of the often-pervasive identifications with the traumatizing other's negating experience and treatment of the patient as a child. It is as if in certain domains of functioning, the patient's only, or at least controlling, experience of self is "through the mind" of the parent, or more accurately, through identification with the child's experience of the parent's mind. I have come to think of this intrapsychic situation as *living in an airless world*. The child or patient, like all of us, has their ongoing primary experience: Winnicott's (1960/1965) "going on being." But, as we know from psychoanalytic theories beginning with Sullivan, Winnicott, Bion, and Kohut, we come into being as a self (or selves) only as a function of the ways we and our primary subjectivities are experienced, interpreted, and responded to by our significant others. There is always our *primary experience* and our *experience of our experience*. In the situation I am describing, the patient's experience of their experience is identified with one or more negating others, and in that sense is "airless." This toxic intrapsychic configuration is associated with a range of serious developmental problems affecting the senses of self and agency and the capacities to think, feel, separate, and grieve.

Because the concept of identification is so strongly associated with Freud's structural model, and classical theory more generally, it tends to be thought of as a vestige of one-person psychology—an internalized "structure" laid down in childhood, then operating throughout life in a relatively fixed, unidirectional, repetitive way. The kind of identification I am focusing on—let's call it, generically, *identification with the other's response to the self*—is not just an aspect of psychological organization; it also can be *a way of functioning*, a potentially problematic way of functioning, which, for some individuals unconsciously dominates their approach to the challenges of life. (See Appendix for a history of the theoretical roots of this type of identification.)

What follows is a condensed version of the complex dynamic underpinnings of life lived in an airless world.[1] It is important to say that these dynamics exist on a continuum of severity. I have found this model to be very helpful, not only with the relatively small group of patients at the extreme end, but with a much larger group who have elements of the syndrome in varying degrees of severity. Indeed, it is not a reach to say that we all have areas or "pockets of airlessness" and experience some form of the dynamic configuration I am about to describe.

Living in an Airless World

Whereas Ferenczi linked his patients' "identifications with the aggressor," and their associated lack of what we now call personal agency, to the trauma of sexual seduction in childhood, the trauma responsible for my patients' psychically airless worlds is typically some form of profound negation by one or both parents, although sexual abuse can also be part of this picture. The parent(s), by dint of their own serious character pathology and legacies of transgenerational trauma, experienced at least this particular child through a lens so distorted by their archaic needs and projections that the patient as a child was never perceived as the person they actually were with the needs and feelings they actually had. Rather, they were experienced and related to as the object their parents perceived or needed them to be, or the child who *failed* to be the object their parents needed them to be.

The developmental result is a latter-day version of Ferenczi's (1933) "confusion of tongues"—there is an inability to discriminate between one's own primary subjective experience (spontaneous affects, perceptions, impulses, needs, desires) and that experience as interpreted and responded to by the internalized, negating other. Stated differently, the predominant experience of self is the *self as object* (Bollas, 1987; Ogden, 1986)—usually a bad, unwanted, or deficient object, though in some cases an overly idealized one—rather than the *self as agentic subject*. (See also Frankel, 2002, pp. 117–125, and Shaw, 2014 for similar developmental accounts.) As a result of this confusion and the invalidation of one's primary experience by the internalized other, the sense of self remains poorly articulated or distorted—usually both—making it less of a resource for navigating the complexities of life. This deficit in turn leads to a distrust in one's own experience and capacities, a tendency to project power and wisdom onto the other, and an addictive-like dependency on the other's perspective, with which one over-identifies. This identificatory bondage *is* a form of relational connection, but it masks a profound *sense of aloneness* stemming from the lack of recognition, originally from the parental other, and later the internalized other. Such aloneness has implications for the *capacity to experience and process affects*. Namely, the overwhelming feelings, thoughts, and memories associated with the original traumas cannot be borne in isolation: They must be shared to be tolerable. And this disability in turn impairs the *capacity to grieve* the damage and losses attendant upon the early traumas.

When I say patients living in airless worlds are impaired in their ability to tolerate the affects associated with their early traumas, this doesn't mean they don't feel things. The patient may well feel hopeless, dead, empty (haunted by feelings of non-being), suicidal, destructively rageful, relentlessly self-hating, shame-ridden, guilty, cynical, envious, or filled with dread and overwhelming anxiety—but these affects are uncontained and toxic such that feeling them, or even having them verbally, empathically recognized, doesn't help, or doesn't help much. They have not yet, as Winnicott (1960/1965) would say, been incorporated into the patient's sphere of omnipotence. In Bionian language, such affects are the equivalent of *beta elements* that have not yet been successfully metabolized by *alpha function* into thinkable, useable feelings (Bion, 1962; Ogden, 2004). As one patient who had begun to move out of her particular airless world put it: "There's crying [about her mother's toxic inadequacies] that feels relieving and crying that feels like disintegrating."

Consequently, for patients still living in airless worlds, the shared recognition of affectivity, either in the self-psychological sense of empathic recognition or in Bromberg's (2011) sense of bi-directional "self-state sharing," may not be the first order of business. The patient's central unconscious need and preoccupation when still in an airless world is *to convert their actual parents into true parents who will finally recognize their subjective experience and needs, thereby allowing them, for the first time, psychically to breathe.* (See also Fairbairn, 1952 and Ogden, 2010.) This is so because the under-developed sense of agency, inability to feel in an integrated way, and inability to grieve have also precluded true separation-individuation, locking the patient into both their real and internalized parents' orbit of reality with no way out.

This understanding has implications for how we think about the so-called analytic field (Baranger & Baranger, 1961–1962/2009). While the dynamic constellation I'm describing may well play out in the transference-counter-transference relationship (i.e., needing the analyst as presumed old, negating object to become the analyst as new, recognizing object), these patients are still very much in the grip of their *developmental parent-child fields* in ways that usually need to be explicitly addressed and worked with, even as they are simultaneously engaging as patients within the analytic field.

Therapeutic Implications

We are used to expecting models of this sort to generate specific principles of therapeutic intervention and action. Dissociation theorists, for example, have generated certain principles for recognizing and transforming enactments (e.g., Mitchell, 1997; Bromberg, 2011; Benjamin, 2018). While the theory of the airless world suggests a number of general clinical principles, I have found that just having the model in mind and seeing how its dynamic permutations play out in different patients' struggles has been what is most helpful. In a way, *not* having a prescriptive approach is exactly what these patients need since their core issue is the impingement of others' mental frameworks on the development of their authentic subjectivity.

Ultimately, the aims of treatment will need to include the patient separating from the internalized, negating other to free themselves for the *re-subjectification* process at the heart of the work. Usually, this capacity to separate will depend on the patient forming a sufficiently deep and trusting (selfobject) connection to the analyst, such that the overwhelming affects and realities associated with the early traumas and losses can be recognized, witnessed, reclaimed, and worked through (grieved). But the specific path toward these process aims—the specific *needed relationship* (S. Stern, 2017)—is always unique and emergent from the complex evolution of the dyadic system over time.

The question of separation-individuation is all-important and requires some elaboration. We tend to think of separation-individuation as an *interpersonal* process that occurs gradually over the course of infancy, childhood, adolescence, and young adulthood. Children gradually, fitfully separate from their caregivers—not totally of course, but enough to have begun the process of developing their own minds and senses of self and personal agency. For adult patients whose psyches have been colonized by, fused with, and disabled by their caregivers in circumscribed but essential ways, this identificatory fusion needs to be "softened" and opened up such that their minds and selves can begin to "breathe" and strengthen. Moreover, the problem is no longer one of simply separating from their parents, even their internalized parents; they must "separate" from a total internalized relational environment, including the various senses of self and other derived from that environment (Bollas, 1987; Mitchell, 1993; Davies, 1996), and all the adaptive and compensatory strategies they were forced to construct and evolve, given the dangers of their early environments and the sometimes profound deficits, vulnerabilities, and deformations in their capacities for self-delineation, agency, and navigation in their relational worlds. These constructions and adaptations exert the same controlling force as the parent of a young child, and one can think of them as integral parts of a self that is still unconsciously tied to the original object through very early identifications with the other's response to the self. Moreover, as part of this same self-organization, in many significant subsequent relationships, including, in some instances, relationships with one's own children, transferences form in which the other seems to exert this same kind of controlling force. In effect, the patient unconsciously cedes to the other the power to define the self, even as they might try consciously to resist this existential influence.

Understanding these vicissitudes of the problem of separation-individu-ation is necessary to grasp the problems with grieving. We tend to think of a grieving process as central to psychological growth in analytic treatment. The patient ultimately will need to *grieve the loss of that which they never had* and all the damage, pain, and suffering caused by profound early rela-tional trauma. But such grieving requires the *capacity* to grieve, which can-not develop so long as the patient's mind and self cannot stand apart from the internalized negating/controlling other. Thus, the beginning of empathy with these patients may be recognizing the impossibility of grieving—a reality that may persist for a very long time.

One difficult lesson I have learned from working with patients suffering from some form of this syndrome is that the identificatory mode of func-tioning illuminated by the model is so deeply, probably neurobiologically, inscribed in the patient's psychic "structure" and ways of organizing expe-rience that extreme respect for its power and tenacity, and extreme patience regarding one's expectations for change, are called for. In his (2012) arti-cle, "The Essence of Psychoanalysis as Opposed to What is Secondary," Neville Symington wisely wrote:

> The *nooumenon* [essence] of psycho-analysis is ***who you are*** and the *phenomena* [secondary supporting structures and processes] are the acts through which I become who I am. ***The process of becoming who I am*** occurs in many different ways. Defining psycho-analysis as the ***process of becoming who I am*** has therefore two components: the ***who I am*** component and the ***process of becoming*** component…I can only become who I am by freeing myself of the chains that imprison me.
>
> (p. 402; emphasis in the original)

I agree with this total statement but would place special emphasis on the last sentence. Because of the deeply inscribed identificatory structures and processes of the sort described in the present chapter, the ***who I am*** cannot readily be recognized and cannot emerge on its own simply by co-creating a space of sufficient freedom and empathic attunement. The identificatory structures and processes must be identified, located historically, and actively *deconstructed* (co-deconstructed) in order to create the potential space for the ***who I am*** to emerge, develop, and begin to be experienced as ***me***.

Patients often put great pressure on themselves to change their relent-less, repetitive, dysfunctional patterns of experiencing and relating.

While virtually all psychoanalytic theories contribute dimensions of under-standing of the complex forces in the personality (the "chains") that make transformation of these patterns so difficult, I have found that the model articulated here has greatly increased my understanding with certain patients, such that they come to feel understood and, in a sense, encouraged by the recognition of both the origins, and reasons for the intractability, of their ways of experiencing.

The understanding that their toxic ways of experiencing themselves in relation to others are simultaneously "of the self" and "not of the self," in the sense of being introjections of alien construals and treatment of the self by reality-defining parental others (Fonagy & Target, 1996), helps explain, and fosters greater compassion toward, their often demoralizing sense of stuckness—imprisonment in both their own minds and the intersubjective knots of their relational worlds. It also offers realistic hope for change, even if painfully slow. The model assumes that in a patient's life there has been, all along, and continues to be, a primary, creative, potential self (Winnicott, 1965). It is not that there is "nothing there" apart from their self-negating attitudes and behaviors. They are not simply "empty," but rather have "sub-stance" which can be "felt" if recognized, and once felt can be developed in a gradual process of "subjectification" (Pinato, Moia, & Negri, 2011; Shaw, 2014).

The dual processes of deconstruction and re-subjectification, in the con-text of a deepening selfobject relationship with the analyst, amount to a slow form of transformational alchemy wherein a patient's core experience of self and self-in-relation-to-others gradually and very fitfully morphs into a new, truer (more reality-based) sense of self grounded in repeated experi-ences of being and feeling recognized and *met* by the therapist, co-creating for the first time, in Louis Sander's (2008) words, a progressive "experi-ence of being known." I think of these necessary analytic conditions as a co-created *medium* that is constantly evolving in unpredictable ways, all in the service of helping the patient resume psychic breathing. This idea has continuities with Benjamin's (2018) concept of a "shared third" that is co-created uniquely over time in analytic dyads. I like the word "medium" because of the implication of many elements interacting simultaneously to create a unique "culture" conducive to the emergence and development of a new sense of self. The word medium also conveys the idea of a liv-ing system—a circumscribed experiential world that the patient and analyst "live in" together. It requires the co-creation of a kind of "life together" to combat the disabling effects of the patient's early prolonged subjection to living in their particular airless world.

Clinical Examples

Identification with Toxic Objectification

Martin, a patient in his late 50s, had been a star athlete as an adolescent and young adult. He won an athletic scholarship to college and clearly showed promise of becoming a professional in one of his chosen sports. Martin's father was a depressed, emotionally limited, narcissistic man whose primary interest in his son was his investment in his son's athletic success. He had no clue about, nor interest in, his son as a person—their relationship was limited to his vicarious enjoyment of his son's athletic accomplishments. Martin, who is also extremely bright, had an emotional breakdown during his freshman year in college, flunked most of his courses, and therefore lost his athletic scholarship, causing him to have to drop out of school. His father was so angry with him that he would not speak to him for six months, and their relationship never really recovered. Martin's athletic career sputtered out and ended in the wake of this crisis.

One of Martin's presenting symptoms was that, throughout his adult life, he had had such a conflicted relationship to his body and athleticism that he had never been able to even work out or stay in reasonable shape, let alone play a sport, since early adulthood. Whatever inherent pleasure or feeling of competence he might originally have experienced from his athletic capacities had been thoroughly toxified and disabled within his relationship with his father. Thus, a major therapeutic aim was to reclaim at least some of his early positive relationship to his body and athletic self. The problem was that within the latter, intersubjectively constructed relationship, his body had been appropriated as an object for the gratification of his father's primitive needs in the context of a total negation of his—the son's—subjectivity. Thus, for Martin to reinvest in his own body was to unconsciously merge or re-identify with this early objectification and negation from which he had never really separated—an experience so toxic that it seemed to preclude any possibility of connecting with his earlier, primary body-self-experience.

Martin had grown up as an object not only of his father's but of both parents' toxic needs (minds). The mother, for her part, implicitly looked to him to serve certain, very precocious, therapist-like functions in the family from middle childhood on. Now, as an adult, he was unconsciously unable to separate himself from the needs of those he was close to. He experienced himself as hopelessly at the mercy of the needs of others, to which he felt more or less compelled to respond. Even though he understood this intellectually, he was powerless to change it on his own. *It was a psychological fact of his existence.* If a person he cared about had a need, especially a need for something he couldn't realistically provide (the position his parents had put him in), he was placed in an impossibly painful situation for which he had no effective coping strategies. We might say that he was completely identified with the expectation that it was his job to respond helpfully to the need of the other. This is a vivid example of what I call identificatory living or living in an airless world. This way of living was so oppressive and enervating for Martin that the only way he had found to cope was to get away from people entirely. His fantasy life consisted primarily of imagining long trips by himself on the road or in the wilderness.

Attachment to Self-Organization

My patient, Anna, who was unloved and carelessly treated by her mother, and whose relationship to her somewhat more engaged father was organized around meeting his needs, grew up feeling a profound sense of isolation and not belonging to the "community" she most needed and wanted to be a part of—her family. There was a childhood depression, which she characterized (and remembered) as feeling like a sad, dull girl, sitting on the couch by herself for hours watching TV. Part of her compensatory adaptation as she grew up was to construct her adult experiential world on the principles of self-improvement, accomplishment, and gaining recognition and acceptance in the social and professional communities she idealized. By the time she began treatment with me in her early 60s, even though she was quite successful in many respects, her subjective world was dominated by feelings of failure and regret—focused on all the mistakes she had made, opportunities she had squandered, and levels of success and recognition she had not achieved. There was a pervading sense of disappointment and hopelessness, and her implicit (and explicit) question for her therapy, and me, was: How could she possibly find happiness at this point, given all these tragic "facts" about her life which could no longer be reversed or rectified?

In a case like this, airless world theory helps illuminate that underneath Anna's adult psychological organization, she was still in part the little girl trapped in a negating relationship with her mother (and to some degree, her father) from which she had never really separated. That unconscious bondage (no space or air) extended to all the adult organizing principles through which she had tried to set up her world on the more ostensibly hopeful premise that she could finally achieve a sense of acceptance and belonging through conditional love—that is, based on her demonstrated capacities, achievements, and appealing qualities. This, of course, was a doomed project because the core problem and source of her depression was the absence of *unconditional* love from her parents.

In therapy, I assumed that ultimately Anna would need to recognize and get space from her unconscious identification with her mother's implicit rejection of her as unlovable and that this would require a new experience with me that gradually counteracted and emancipated her from this archaic, oppressive relationship to herself. This involved (1) an empathic, sometimes playfully argumentative, confrontation and deconstruction of her conscious quest for redemption via her efforts to meet certain success criteria; (2) a stubborn (often felt as clichéd and boring) insistence on my part that the underlying problem still resided in her early, internalized relationships with her parents and negative identifications grounded in those relationships; and (3) a gradual demonstration of my authentic, (relatively) unconditional love—i.e., a love that did not expect or require her to be a good, interesting (not dull), affirming patient. This last part was easy since Anna and I genuinely liked and enjoyed each other, and I never found her dull, even in her most flattened, depressed states.

Crucially, the living frame (Goldberg, 2018) for this work was the close tracking of Anna's deepening selfobject transference and her tendency to dissociate from it, given her life-long distrust and cynicism regarding intimate, dependent relationships and consequent compensatory pattern of privileging more external failure and success criteria. A repeated subtle enactment, given that I had some similar tendencies, was that *both* of us could become caught up with more external preoccupations, to the neglect of the mostly unconscious impact on Anna's moods and states of her current experience of my engagement with her. When we drifted away from a primary focus on our connection for too long, or had too long a break, she slowly sank back into her depressive pessimism. Yet, as soon as we caught this drifting-away tendency and refocused on her current experience of me

and us, there was an almost-immediate restoration of a more vital, confident, hopeful, happier self-state. An important moment in the treatment
occurred when Anna, on her own, recognized this sequence for the first
time and made the self-interpretation (Winnicott, 1969, p. 86) that it signified my genuine, un-prompted attentiveness to her well-being.

There is a more general point here about patients' tendency to regress
during long breaks or periods of felt disconnection. Each major psychoanalytic theory has its own explanation(s) for such decompensations. Airless
world theory suggests that as the new selfobject relationship with the analyst acquires increasing power to counteract the old, unconscious, controlling identifications with the other's response to the self, separations and
derailments that temporarily weaken this counteracting effect *throw the
patient back onto/into the still-extremely-powerful controlling force of the
old object relationships and their identificatory prison*, gradually eroding
any degree of agency and well-being that has accrued from the new selfobject connection.

While Anna's struggles lay at the healthier end of the airless world continuum, there was a core area of emotional imprisonment that had been
impervious to a previous, in many ways helpful, psychoanalytic treatment.
The theory of the airless world helped me understand her inability to separate from and grieve the sources of her deep feelings of worthlessness,
hopelessness, and unlovability, which were masked by more conscious
feelings of failure, regret, and shame. The yield of this understanding was
that Anna increasingly grounded her personal aims (and criteria for happiness) in her true interests, desires, andcapacities, and the realities of her
present life.

The Complex Relationship Between Identification and Dissociation

Liz was a bright, competent woman in her late 30s who functioned in a
capable, energetic, if somewhat worried and preoccupied way much of
the time. However, she was susceptible to extreme state shifts linked to
her perception of happenings in her important relationships. She looked
to others for a kind of mirroring that included both accurate reflection and
validating acceptance. When she experienced others as seeing her as something she wasn't, needing her to be something she wasn't, or rejecting her,
especially out of apparent preference for some third party, she would be

thrown into a traumatized state of extreme depressive anxiety and preoccupation which she was helpless to get out of by herself. We were able to
connect these reactive states to similar states she had experienced as a child
with her mother, whom Liz had experienced as often not there for her emotionally, criticizing her for being negative and hyper-sensitive, and prefer-
ring Liz's younger sister. My sense was that there was also a split in the
mother's personality, the dark side of which had a primitive, unconsciously
destructive edge, and that, for complex reasons, Liz had been the target of
her mother's "bad object" projections.

Much could be said about Liz's struggle, but the point I want to emphasize
is that her early experience made her susceptible to a form of involuntary
identification with the responses of others that were in any way reminis-
cent of her mother's treatment of her *and*, at the same time, rendered her
intolerably, frighteningly alone. Not surprisingly, this still occurred with
her mother, with whom Liz maintained a close if ambivalent relationship.
In fact, some of Liz's most debilitating decompensations occurred during
prolonged visits with her mother over summer vacations.

Early in our work, when Liz was in her depressed, fragmented state,
she looked to me with a kind of desperation to soothe her and help her try
to understand what was happening to her. Because her state shifts were
so clearly illuminated by the theory of the airless world, I was often able
to offer her empathic (though sometimes long-winded) explanations with
which she resonated; and when it worked, she would feel dramatically
relieved and calmed and was able to re-enter her more "normal," positive,
energetic state. However, within this positive state her entire focus became
one of avoiding re-entering the other state and urgently needing to view
herself as the more normal person she felt herself to be in this healthier
state. Within this mode, her focus became one of finding positive self-help
strategies she could use to strengthen herself and give her tools for prevent-
ing or managing the other fragmented state. In this mode, she looked to me
for validation of her strength and basic health, wanted me to get on board
with helping her develop self-help skills, and resisted any suggestion that
addressing her deeper vulnerability would require longer-term treatment.
In fact, Liz broke off treatment twice before becoming convinced that she
needed more intensive therapy.

As she allowed me to become more important to her, Liz became highly
vigilant regarding my every facial expression and bit of verbal feedback,
continuously scanning my responses for evidence of my disposition toward

her and identifying (mostly unconsciously) with her perception and interpretation of my disposition (exactly as Ferenczi had found with his traumatized patients). Note here the fluid relationship between identification
as an intersubjective process in the here and now, and identification as an
internalized, relatively fixed disposition toward oneself. If Liz experienced
me as misperceiving, judging, or abandoning her, she became intensely
preoccupied and distant—simultaneously adopting (what she inferred to
be) my viewpoint as her own (namely that she was defective and worthy of
rejection) while trying to defend herself against my influence. Within this
identification she became fused with, yet alienated from, me, and at the
same time alienated from her authentic self-experience and needs, leaving
her alone, fragmented, and panicked.

If Liz remained in one of these fragmented states for more than a few
sessions, she would become increasingly distant and angry, frustrated that I
wasn't giving her more concrete tools for calming herself, and paranoid that
maybe I was not the person she should trust to help her. At these times, I got
more than a taste of what I assumed was the threatening, ruthless quality in
the mother's more destructive attitudes toward Liz—the aggressive side of
Liz's identification with the aggressor.

In these ominous, escalating disconnects, it felt like I needed to work
hard to maintain enough calm, presence of mind, and reflective capacity to
be able to withstand the pressure and keep processing what was happening.
If I was able to do this and reach an understanding of what had initially
triggered Liz's alienation (usually something with either her mother or me),
she would quickly calm down and express gratitude for my non-judgmental
steadiness and commitment, especially in light of the fact that, in her words,
"I know I'm not easy!" There were times, however, when I was not able
to maintain my cool, and things would devolve into enactments wherein
her angry, paranoid distancing operations prompted a reciprocal passive-
aggressive disengagement on my part—creating an unspoken feeling in the
room that the relationship might be coming undone.

Did these enactments reflect a mutual dissociation process, as posited
by multiple-self-state theory (e.g., D.B. Stern, 2010; Bromberg, 2011)?
In part, yes: I think Liz was dissociating her intense dependent needs,
abandonment panic, narcissistic injury, and reactive rage in relation to
me; and I was struggling with my own dissociated anger and attachment
vulnerabilities. But I find it more useful to combine this awareness with

the additional understanding that such enactments re-create an airless world in the transference-countertransference relationship, wherein both parties are unconsciously identifying with the other's ostensibly negating, rejecting attitude, thereby disabling the analyst's containing function and the collaborative containing function of the patient/analyst system (Cooper, 2000). This is, of course, the kind of dynamic Benjamin (2004, 2018) has brilliantly characterized as a "doer/done-to complementarity" and the loss of "thirdness." What airless world theory adds to this formulation is the understanding that each party brings their "pockets of airlessness" into the interaction, unconsciously identifying with the other's negating treatment, and shifting into a child-like (unconsciously dependent) transference state in which the other's recognition and love seem to become the sole and necessary source of psychic air and self-restoration. This situation, once fully engaged, can preclude the kind of separation necessary to resolve such deadlocks, which requires the capacity, first in the analyst, to *recognize, accept, and potentially grieve what the other is not (and may not be able to be), and what we have not been (and may not be able to be) for the other*.

A turning point in the treatment came during one especially prolonged enactment in our fourth year of work for which we were unable to locate any plausible initial trigger. Liz's participation in our sessions felt increasingly like she was going through the motions, not talking about anything that felt immediate or compelling. I could feel a subtle sense of impatience or irritability growing, but she denied anything was wrong, or at least anything that she could account for. There was a distinct sense that our relationship was fraying, and I felt helpless to do anything about it. The enactment had not resolved before Liz left on her usual month-long summer break. During that break, I had the sinking feeling that she would come back and tell me she was ending treatment, and that this would have a very frustrated, critical, angry edge. Thus, I was preoccupied with and dreading her return until about two days prior to our resumption of sessions. As it approached, I became aware of feeling very angry myself. I got in touch with the feeling that whatever had prompted Liz's disengagement, I had done nothing so terribly wrong—at least not intentionally or within my awareness; thus, her anger, which I could sense was there, seemed unfair. I had fantasies of expressing this anger to her directly but knew this would only make matters worse. Then, in the last 24 hours before our first session back, these feelings transmuted into a new sense of conviction that anger and rage were pervading the treatment under the surface, and that the anger needed somehow to become an "object of analysis" as Ogden (1994), following Green (1975), would say. Along with this realization came a confident sense that our treatment was not yet over; yet, paradoxically, this confidence was coupled with an acceptance that Liz might be too far gone—that I might lose her and have to grieve the loss of a patient who had become important to me.

Whatever feelings Liz had been approaching our first session with, I'm sure that when she arrived, she could sense a shift had taken place in me. Thus, even before I said anything, one could feel the tension between us subsiding quickly. In that session, I was able to name the anger that both of us had been feeling and say that this seemed to be an area that was important to look at and work on together. Liz seemed relieved and reassured by this direct, more confident approach and agreed fully that anger was an issue for her and that our work was not yet done. It seemed that my having first contained my own anger, then naming anger as an analytic object, contained the anger "in the room"; psychic air had thereby been reintroduced into our temporarily airless analytic field, and we both regained the capacity to "think" about what we were feeling. In retrospect, I could see that this enactment and its resolution proved so powerful because uncontained, dissociated anger had been a transgenerational problem in Liz's family, evident in the mother's inexplicable unconscious destructiveness directed toward Liz. It had also been a problem in my family, where my experience had sensitized me to situations of periodic, sometimes prolonged, anger (and apparent withdrawal of love) that could not be processed or mentalized through dialogue.

As potentially threatening, and ultimately important to the treatment process, as our enactments were, I do not see them as the main story of our transformative work during Liz's five-year treatment. Initially, much of our attention was focused on her outside relationships, especially that with her mother. She gradually came to understand in an actionable way—that is, with real emotional depth and a newfound sense of agency—the nature and reasons for her vulnerability to emotional fragmentation, and came to be able to recognize, and get space from, the subtly negating ways that her mother *still* acted toward her and affected her. As things improved with her mother, the focus shifted to our relationship and the dramatic swings in her (transference) experience of me as often helpful, calming, understanding, and fully accepting of her, but sometimes the opposite of these qualities. I regard these swings as a complex form of selfobject transference wherein only over time, many tests, and many rupture-and-repair sequences did her confidence in my understanding and liking of *her*, and hence her confidence in her own goodness and lovability and in her own sense of reality, grow stronger. Our journey was a bit tumultuous from beginning to end—a tumult that Liz seemed to need me to experience and survive. But in the end, she had internalized a new experience of recognition and (relatively) unconditional acceptance that effectively combated her "identifications with negation," making her less prone to fragmentation, and less in need of her dissociative defense.

A Complex Model of the Relationally Traumatized Mind

I chose Liz for my extended example because her personality organization demonstrates one version of the relationship between the dissociative divisions of multiple-self-state theory and the toxic identifications implicated in the theory of the airless world. Liz's two very different self-states were certainly kept separate by rigid dissociation. But this understanding, while clinically apt and useful, doesn't capture the crux of Liz's susceptibility to fragmentation and isolation. This can only be grasped as a function of the "airlessness" of her unconscious identification with the primitive, unloving, and negating side of her mother's attitude toward her as a child. How, then, to characterize both the intrapsychic and theoretical relationship between identification and dissociation? It gets complicated because, if we take Philip Bromberg's version of dissociation theory, he is clearly aware of major elements of the dynamics I have described. But his narrative becomes confusing when he tries to fit them all into a theory of dissociation. Bromberg (2011) writes:

> the way any person is seen in the mind of an "other" must reflect the core self that was "his parent's child"...[The] relational patterns defining the core self are built upon, modified, and integrated into a configuration of individuality that is largely non-dissociative. However, if parts of the self were systematically disconfirmed early in life, the task of continuing to exist in the mind of another person (and thereby his own eyes) as the same self that was "his parent's child" is

a much more complicated and difficult task because it includes having to dissociate those self-states that are disjunctive with it. Those parts tend to remain cognitively unsymbolized…[These] "not-me" parts of the self must become amenable to self-reflection by being cognitively and linguistically symbolized in a relational context before they can become part of what the person feels as "me." Until that happens, the "not-me" parts continue to hang around and enact dissociatively what cannot be thought or said, making trouble both for the patient and for people in his life.

(p. 58)

I would argue that, while there are profound clinical and etiological insights in this account, Bromberg's overall conceptualization suffers from trying to fold all of the psychic phenomena he is observing into a dissociation-based mental model rather than one that recognizes the complex interaction between identification and dissociation. With the kinds of patients he is describing, the problem is not simply that some parts of the self were confirmed and others disconfirmed, and therefore dissociated. The problem with Liz, for example, was that *most* of the self was *mis-represented* or, if you will, *mis-mentalized* in highly pejorative and toxic ways, such that what Bromberg is calling the "core self," or Liz's dominant experience of "me," was the major reason for her confusion of tongues and source of traumatic agitation. What caused Liz to fragment was the identificatory re-activation of toxic experiences embedded in this dominant self, which I actually don't think of as the core self. Her core self resided in her primary needs for recognition, acceptance, affirmation, and affect regulation; her vulnerability to fragmentation; her traumatically overwhelming reactive affects of panic, isolation, rage, and fight/flight impulses; and in her slowly strengthening reflective and self-regulatory capacities, sense of personal agency, confidence in her sense of reality, and feelings of lovability as our work together deepened and progressed.

I think the question of what exactly gets dissociated and why is highly complex and probably unique in each case, as is the question of what is "me" and "not me." But the main problem I see with Bromberg's and other similar models is that dissociation of whatever kind is only part of a larger, more complex picture. Dissociation, by its nature and definition, is a segment of self-experience and/or overwhelming affect that has been split off from the dominant self, however the dominant self is envisioned. What airless world theory makes clear is that it is the whole self-organization, including the dominant self and the dissociated self-states, that is the source of difficulty. Dissociation may mark the fault lines, and the working through of enactments may be necessary to heal them. But the deconstruction and re-subjectification of the dominant self is often the larger, longer project. Actually, the fuller statement would be: (1) that dissociation and identification are two complexly inter-related dimensions of the relationally traumatized self; and (2) that the theories of both dynamics, and their complex interactions, are necessary for the understanding and treatment of airless world problems.

Conclusion: Proximity to Neighboring Theories

My aim in this first chapter has been to make the case for a more complex, relationally grounded model of the (traumatically altered) mind—one that more fully takes into account the identificatory as well as the dissociative sequelae, originally identified by Ferenczi (1933), which arise from certain kinds of profound early relational trauma. Aspects of this model and the phenomena it describes bear similarities to concepts in a number of neighboring models and theories.

First among these is Bernard Brandchaft's (1994; Brandchaft et al., 2010) "systems of pathological accommodation." Brandchaft insightfully portrayed the intrapsychic situation when parents override or negate their children's psychic realities in various ways, implicitly requiring the child to adopt the parent's reality as a condition for approval and acceptance in the attachment relationship. That is, the child learns to *accommodate* the parent's reality, values, and judgments lest they lose the needed attachment. There are significant homologies between Brandchaft's theory of pathological accommodation and mine of identification with the other's response to the self; but the two phenomena are not the same. This is most clearly demonstrated by patients at the extreme end of the airless world continuum where, beginning from birth, the child is experienced and treated by the parent as a certain kind of object, such that the parent's experience of the child is the only way the child has ever experienced themself.

My patient Elizabeth (not to be confused with Liz) had been unwanted by a nearly psychotic mother and was treated by the mother throughout her entire childhood and adolescence as an emotional and financial burden. For example, she was not taken to the hospital with acute appendicitis, almost causing her death. Later she was given the message by the father that the reason he was sexually abusing her rather than her sisters was that she looked like a dog. Elizabeth completely and inescapably identified with these parental registrations, such that today, after 40 years of analytic treatment, many transformative changes, and a reasonably full and successful life, she still is vulnerable to feeling like a worthless, undeserving human, to obsessing about any imposition she places on others in order to get her own needs met, and to reflexively identifying (although not nearly to the same degree) with any communication from another person she takes to be an implicit judgment of her inadequacies. I don't think of this as a pathological accommodation (although for many years she did that too—the two often go hand in hand). I think of it as an inescapable form of primary identification (Stern, 2002a; b) within which there is no space, no air, between her never-recognized, under-developed potential self and the self her parents construed her to be.

Brandchaft and I are (were) both trying to get at the nature and causes of very similar and, in many ways, overlapping phenomena. These cases are always complex, and any single theory is necessarily an oversimplification. It often requires both of our theories to grasp the vicissitudes of these patients' "imprisonment within the gulags of their minds" (Brandchaft, 1994), and/or life lived within their particular airless worlds.

In addition to its links with Brandchaft's theory of pathological accommodation, certain features of what I am calling airless world syndrome correspond to aspects of Klein's (1946) "paranoid-schizoid position," especially as re-interpreted by Ogden (1986), and to Lacan's (1977) "identification with the other's desire" (see Fink, 1997). Certain other features, as I have noted, are covered in Benjamin's (2004, 2018) theory of "doer/done-to complementarity," while still others are recognized in Eigen's (1999) seminal work on "toxic nourishment." Shaw's (2014) insightful rendering of the "relational systems of subjugation" created in families dominated by malignant narcissists connects in significant ways with my theory of the airless world, as does Shengold's (1989) early account of the phenomenon of "soul murder." Finally, and importantly, Gerson's (2009) concept of the "dead third"—the psychological sequelae when a culture fails to recognize and bear witness to the devastating lasting impact of genocide or comparable social atrocities—could be described as an airless world writ large, with very similar intrapsychic consequences.

All of these theorists have sought to understand (so as to be better able to treat) patients with powerfully negating and destructive *relationships to themselves*, grounded in (sometimes subtly) destructive early relational systems that may or may not have featured manifest sexual, physical, or verbal abuse, or gross neglect. Airless world theory recontextualizes many of these common features within a distinct paradigm emphasizing the developmental and intrapsychic vicissitudes of early identifications with parental negation. I have found that this theory, held loosely, helps to illuminate the complex intrapsychic and intersubjective worlds characteristic of this historically refractory group of relationally traumatized patients, such that, to paraphrase Winnicott: When they look, they are seen, and thus, for the first time, begin to feel that they exist.

Note

1 Throughout the remainder of this chapter, I use various terms to refer to the collection of clinical observations and conceptual formulations that constitute the group of ideas I am organizing under the rubric "living in an airless world." At different points, I call it a "model," a "syndrome," a "theory," and a "paradigm." Probably the most accurate characterization would be to describe it as a particular *conceptual lens* or *frame of reference*, or, to use Bion's term, a *vertex* through which a certain group of related psychic phenomena are illuminated and organized in a new and clinically useful way. It is also intended to be an evocative metaphor that captures the phenomenological quality of intrapsychic life that follows from a childhood defined by the experience of pervasive parental negation. Many of the elements of this model derive from or overlap with elements from other psychoanalytic frames of reference; and the model as a whole has convergences with "neighboring" theories, some of which I explicitly recognize throughout the chapter, especially in the concluding section.

References

Baranger, M., & Baranger, W. (1961–1962/2009). The analytic situation as a dynamic field. *International Journal of Psychoanalysis*, *89*, 795–826.

Benjamin, J. (2004). Beyond doer and done to: An intersubjective view of thirdness. *Psychoanalytic Quarterly*, *73*: 5–46.

Benjamin, J. (2018). *Beyond doer and done to: Recognition theory, intersubjectivity and the third.* London and New York, NY: Routledge.

Bion, W.R. (1962). *Learning from experience.* London: Heinemann.

Bollas, C. (1987). *Shadow of the object.* New York, NY: Columbia University Press.

Brandchaft, B. (1994). To free the spirit from its cell. In R.D. Stolorow, G.E. Atwood, & B. Brandchaft (Eds.), *The intersubjective perspective* (pp. 57–76). Northvale, NJ: Jason Aronson.

Brandchaft, B., Doctors, S., & Sorter, D. (2010). *Toward an emancipatory psychoanalysis: Brandchaft's intersubjective vision.* New York, NY and London: Routledge.

Bromberg, P.M. (2011). *The shadow of the tsunami and the growth of the relational mind.* New York, NY and London: Routeledge.

Cooper, S.H. (2000). Mutual containment in the analytic situation. *Psychoanalytic Dialogues, 10*: 169–194.

Davies, J.M. (1996). Linking the "pre-analytic" with the postclassical: Integration, dissociation, and the multiplicity of unconscious process. *Contemporary Psychoanalysis, 32*: 553–576.

Eigen, M. (1999). *Toxic nourishment.* London: Karnac Books.

Fairbairn, W.R.D. (1952). *An object-relations theory of the personality.* New York, NY: Basic Books.

Ferenczi, S. (1933). Confusion of tongues between adults and children: The language of tenderness and passion (M. Balint, Ed.) *International Journal of Psycho-Analysis, 30*: 1949.

Fink, B. (1997). *A clinical introduction to Lacanian psychoanalysis: Theory and technique.* Cambridge, MA: Harvard University Press.

Fonagy, P., & Target, M. (1996). Playing with reality: I. Theory of mind and the normal development of psychic reality. *International Journal of Psycho-Analysis, 77*: 217–234.

Frankel, J. (2002). Exploring Ferenczi's concept of identification with the aggressor: Its role in trauma, everyday life, and the therapeutic relationship. *Psychoanalytic Dialogues, 12*: 101–140.

Gerson, S. (2009). When the third is dead: Memory, mourning, and witnessing in the aftermath of the Holocaust. *International Journal of Psychoanalysis, 90*: 1341–1357.

Goldberg, P.L. (2018). *The vital dimension of the frame.* Paper given at the National Meeting of the American Psychoanalytic Association, New York, NY, February 14–18.

Green, A. (1975). The analyst, symbolization, and absence in the analytic setting (On changes in analytic practice and analytic experience). *International Journal of Psycho-Analysis, 43*: 436–440.

Howell, E. (2014). Ferenczi's concept of identification with the aggressor: Understanding dissociative structure with interacting victim and abuser self-states. *American Journal of Psychoanalysis, 74*: 48–59.

Klein, M. (1946). Notes on some schizoid mechanisms. In M. Klein (Ed.), *Envy and gratitude and other works, 1946–1963* (pp. 1–24). New York, NY: Delacorte.

Lacan, J. (1977). *Ecrits: A selection.* New York, NY: W.W. Norton.

Mitchell, S.A. (1993). Multiple selves, singular self. In S.A. Mitchell (Ed.), *Hope and dread in psychoanalysis* (pp. 95–122). New York, NY: Basic Books.

Mitchell, S.A. (1997). *Influence and autonomy in psychoanalysis.* Hillsdale, NJ: The Analytic Press.

Ogden, T.H. (1986). *The matrix of the mind: Object relations and the psychoanalytic dialogue.* Northvale, NJ: Aronson; London: Karnac.
Ogden, T.H. (1994). *Subjects of analysis.* Northvale, NJ: Jason Aronson.
Ogden, T.H. (2004). An introduction to the reading of Bion. *International Journal of Psychoanalysis, 85*: 285–300.
Ogden, T.H. (2010). Why read Fairbairn? *International Journal of Psychoanalysis, 91*: 101–118.
Pinato, M., Moia, A., & Negri, I. (2012). Figures of understanding: The process of image subjectifcation. *International Journal of Psychoanalytic Self Psychology, 7*: 45–68.
Pizer, S. (1998). *Building bridges: The negotiation of paradox in psychoanalysis.* Hillsdale, NJ: The Analytic Press.
Sander, L. (2008). *Living systems, evolving consciousness, and the emerging person: A selection of papers from the life work of Louis Sander* (G. Amadei & I. Bianchi, Eds.). New York, NY and London: Routledge.
Schore, A. (2011). Foreward. In P. Bromberg (Ed.), *The shadow of the tsunami and the growth of the relational mind.* New York, NY and London: Routeledge.
Shaw, D. (2014). *Traumatic narcissism: Relational systems of subjugation.* New York, NY: Routledge.
Shengold, L. (1989). *Soul murder: The effects of childhood abuse and deprivation.* New York, NY: Fawcett Columbine.
Stern, D.B. (2010). *Partners in thought: Working with unformulated experience, dissociation and enactment.* New York, NY and London: Routeledge.
Stern, S. (2002a). The self as a relational structure: A dialogue with multiple-self theory. *Psychoanalytic Dialogues, 12*: 693–714.
Stern, S. (2002b). Identification, repetition, and psychological growth: An expansion of relational theory. *Psychoanalytic Psychology, 19*: 722–738.
Stern, S. (2017). *Needed relationships and psychoanalytic healing: A holistic relational perspective on the therapeutic process.* London and New York, NY: Routledge.
Stern S. (2019). Airless worlds: The traumatic sequelae of identification with parental negation. *Psychoanalytic Dialogues, 29*: 435–450.
Sullivan, H.S. (1953). *The interpersonal theory of psychiatry.* New York, NY: Norton.
Symington, N. (2012). The essence of psycho-analysis as opposed to what is secondary. *Psychoanaltytic Dialogues, 22*: 395–409.
Winnicott, D.W. (1960/1965). The theory of the parent-infant relationship. In D.W. Winnicott (Ed.), *The maturational processes and the facilitating environment* (pp. 37–55). New York, NY: International Universities Press.
Winnicott, D.W. (1969). The use of an object and relating through identifications. In D.W. Winnicott (Ed.), *Playing and reality* (pp. 86–94). London: Tavistock Publications.

Chapter 2

Airless Worlds, Needed Relationships, and Complex Selfobjects

This chapter and the next get into the weeds of the kinds of clinical process through which patients suffering from airless world syndrome can be helped to liberate themselves from their psychic captivities. I will focus on five major principles or constructs as applied in the three clinical examples that constitute this section of the book. The first four are *deconstruction (or co-deconstruction), re-subjectification, the needed relationship*, and *complex selfobjects*. The needed relationship is the primary orienting principle. Deconstruction and re-subjectification are central elements of the needed relationship with airless world patients. A complex selfobject connection is the yield of the needed relationship as it evolves over time and is central to the transformational process. *Breathing together* is a more phenomenological characterization of the emergence of complex selfobject connectedness and will be the focus of Chapter 3.

Martha and the Intractability of Identificatory Bonds

One of the main ways the airless worlds model is helpful is the light it sheds on the seeming intractability of the toxic, disabling, early identifications that the model highlights. For most airless world patients, these identifications began forming at an age when their parents were still held in the idealized position of being the absolute arbiters of truth and reality. Moreover, because the parents' views and treatment of the child were so negating, implicitly or explicitly, of the child's nascent subjectivity, there was little space for that potential self to develop and become integrated through parental attunement, mirroring, and mediation between the child and their relational world. Instead, a kind of occupation took place wherein the child became bound to the parent without the resources to separate and free themselves from that internalized familial prison.

DOI: 10.4324/9781003585237-3

Here is an example. Martha's parents (especially her mother) had shamed and attacked her throughout her childhood and adolescence for any expression of intense affect, positive or negative. As a result, she developed that same relationship to herself. Even after more than ten years of analysis and much progress, when Martha begins to experience very intense affects in session, she reflexively judges these as "stupid," bad, and dangerous and immediately shuts them down, becoming very angry with herself for having them at all. She also assumes, though we have worked through these issues many times, that I will not welcome her feelings and in fact may well attack her in some way for expressing them. Thus, if, as has happened more often in recent years because of the progress she *has* made, she begins to get in touch with the profound sadness of her aloneness as a child such that she feels on the verge of tears, she reflexively develops a headache, which she describes as her involuntary erection of an invisible wall inside her head that keeps the feelings contained and defends against any risk of surrendering to them. Martha's adult self knows that her fears are unwarranted. She has learned to trust me more and more over the years and wants to let down these inner barriers to full connection with me and with her own emotional self. Even so, there remains a core relation to self, or at least to her most deeply emotional self, that is essentially an identificatory formation that she has not been able, or felt ready, to let go of. In the area of emotional experience and expressivity she remains the little girl or young adolescent, trapped in the airless world her parents imposed on her, still unable to separate from them sufficiently to claim her own relation to her authentic emotional experience.

I believe that inner structure will ultimately only yield through Martha's relationship with me, but the question is: How to think about what she needs from me for that transformation to take place? In Chapter 1 I proposed two general categories of intervention: *deconstruction* and *re-subjectification*, both of which are relevant to Martha and have been part of her treatment. Yet these processes cannot simply be applied. They must emerge within the unique *needed relationship* (Stern, 2017) that forms over time with each patient—a co-created space that, hopefully, becomes increasingly "breathable" for the patient.

At this point, I need to take a detour before coming back to Martha. I need to say something about needed relationships and introduce my idea of a *complex selfobject*.

Needed Relationships

What do I mean by the "needed relationship?" It could seem like a truism or tautology—like how someone might characterize any effective psychotherapy. In fact, it is a more meaningful term, one which I spent an entire book (Stern, 2017) trying to unpack. As mentioned in the Introduction to this book, my book on needed relationships implicitly posed the meta-theoretical question: *What level of constructs do we need to be using to think complexly enough about the problem of how we fit what we do clinically to what each patient needs?* The idea of needed relationship seemed to me to be one such construct. It gathers into itself the evolution of psychoanalytic thinking about what our patients need from us. But it is not limited by our theories, in that it also implies holding our theoretical frameworks in the background as we seek to grasp in a specific way what each patient needs from us—both in a given analytic moment and cumulatively over time. What we find they need may not fit easily within pre-existing categories of analytic understanding and participation. In that sense, each needed relationship is more patient-driven or dyad-driven than theory-driven and is essentially improvisational.

My thinking about needed relationships has been influenced by Louis Sander's (2008) principles of facilitative mother–infant interaction (see Stern, 2017, Chapter 1). Sander, a developmental researcher and complex systems thinker, identified a nonlinear relational process of collaboration and coordination between a good-enough mother and infant through which the two partners in the dyad tended naturally to move toward a progressive *fittedness* (his term), enabling the mother to respond to the child's state or need of the moment in such a way that the child feels *met* and thereby helped with the problem or task at hand. One can feel Winnicott hovering in the background of Sander's thinking—an influence he frequently acknowledged. Sander had several terms for capturing this collaborative process: *moments of meeting, relational fittedness, specificity of recognition,* and *specificity of connection.* Here, in a single elegant quote, is the essence of what I find so valuable in Sander's formulations.

> I am asking, "Why not begin with uniqueness as a central principle in the organization of a living system?" I suggest further that specificity of recognition of that uniqueness—in an interactive system—is key to an organizing process based on constructing the essential specificity of connection

between the components that is necessary to achieve the coherence or wholeness of the system required for the continuity of its life.

(2008, p. 226)

I want to highlight Sander's linked processes of specificity of recognition and specificity of connection. I regard these two processes as *interdependent*, *emergent*, and *progressive* within the nonlinear dynamic system of the analytic relationship as it evolves over time. Both evolve toward increasing complexity in their grasp of and response to who the patient is and the nature of their struggles and therapeutic needs. Specificity of recognition is the more familiar idea—mainly from Jessica Benjamin's (1990, 2002, 2004, 2018) work on recognition and mutual recognition, some of which was also influenced by Sander's thinking. It is also close to, though not exactly the same as, the self-psychological idea of empathic resonance (See McKay's [2019] distinction between the two concepts). Specificity of connection has not been so clearly defined or theorized—though Winnicott (1962/1965) came close with his idea that the analyst, like a good-enough mother, needs to make a "live adaptation" to each patient's needs. It implies recognizing not only what the patient is *experiencing in the moment* but what they *need relationally* to move forward. This includes *needs they may not be aware of having until the analyst recognizes them*. Specificity of connection encompasses all the complex and nuanced ways that we learn to *relate* to a given patient—a progressive *contouring* of our ways of being, speaking, and even thinking that is always evolving and adapting to who the patient is and what they need from us.

Finally, like Sander, I situate my approach within a complexity sensibility, as I have come to understand it from the pathbreaking work of Galatzer-Levy (2002, 2017), Stolorow (1997), Coburn (2014), Harris (2005), Marks-Tarlow (2008), and others. The way I would put it is that there is always a dialectical movement going on within the analyst between two kinds of orientation to the process. One involves a more-or-less conscious intention to grasp what the patient needs from us—to work to achieve specificity of recognition and connection, whatever that might mean at a given point in time. The second is a less conscious freedom or surrender through which we allow ourselves to be carried, or rather recognize that we *are* being carried, like it or not, by the ever-changing movement of the system as a whole in which what we feel, think, say, or do at a given point is not simply an expression of our autonomous, conscious (or even unconscious) intention but rather of something that is *emergent* from the entire complex system or field that includes us. I view these two orientations as existing in dialectical relation to each other in the sense that they are mutually constituting and "need" each other (Hoffman, 1998). Thus, we are best served by creating a space within ourselves that is comfortable with the paradoxes they create in our ways of being present.

The Idea of a Complex Selfobject

In the clinical examples I described in my 2019 paper (Chapter 1), I noted that a core element of the treatment had been *the selfobject dimension* of the relationship, although the nature of the selfobject connection was quite different in the two cases. I now have greater clarity about the nature and functioning of this selfobject dimension.

To review briefly: What makes the selfobject idea unique among relational theories is that it posits a forward edge motivational tendency within many patients that, mostly unconsciously, causes the patient to seek, or at least need, certain qualities, functions, or capacities in the therapist. If these capacities are found and fully engaged with, a forward-striving developmental process is set in motion that is a natural and automatic byproduct of that form of relational connection.

Kohut (1971, 1977) identified three primary self-selfobject integrations—mirroring, idealizing, and twinship—which he regarded as somewhat distinct forms of transference that arose in treatment as a function of both the patient's early relational history and the analytic situation, which, by its nature, invites such transferences. (See Strozier et al., 2022, for a succinct review of Kohut's selfobject theory.) Since Kohut, the original concept has broadened considerably. There have been creative elaborations of Kohut's original selfobject categories, such as the important work of Togashi and Kottler (2015) in the area of twinship and alter-ego experiences. There have been additional proposed *types* of selfobject transference, such as Stolorow and Atwood's (1992) "self-delineating selfobject transference." But the concept has also simply expanded to denote a more general dimension of the transference: as in Stolorow, Brandchaft, and Atwood's (1987) "selfobject dimension of the transference" and Marian Tolpin's (2002) "forward edge transferences." These formulations move in the direction of viewing the selfobject dimension of the analytic relationship as organized and evolving in specific and unique ways with each patient.

My thinking about it takes off from these more general formulations. I now view the selfobject dimension of the relationship as highly specific to each patient in whom such a transference arises. I view it as tied to the specific nature of the original relational traumas that make treatment necessary and, also, as specifically fitted to the patient's psychological organization, or subjective world, as it was shaped, in part, by that original trauma and plays out in the analytic relationship and the patient's current life. Moreover, I see it as co-created in the sense that the selfobject connection that develops takes its unique form from the contributions of both parties as they interact over time. Here, the evolution of the selfobject connection, in a given treatment, begins to merge with my idea of the needed relationship, although they are not the same thing. The way I would put it is that, *as the needed relationship develops over time, becoming increasingly fitted to the patient in the context of their unique dyad, the patient's experience of the analyst as a transformative selfobject becomes more fully actualized.* The needed relationship refers to *what we do* with the patient; the selfobject dimension refers to *how the patient experiences what we do*, or at least certain aspects of what we do. Thus, although there may well be some degree of selfobject connection beginning more-or-less automatically early in treatment, it is only with the progressive specificity and complexity of the needed relationship that the selfobject dimension fully emerges as a transformative dynamic.

Airless Worlds and Complex Selfobjects

Kohut (1977) famously likened the psychological need for empathic resonance (and, by implication, selfobject relations) to the physical need for oxygen. What he did not quite see, or at least didn't explicitly write about, was that, with patients like the ones I'm focusing on, there is a two-fold developmental problem that has implications for *the kind* of selfobject relationship that our developmentally traumatized patients require. I alluded to this briefly in Chapter 1, in the section "Living in an Airless World":

(T)he predominant experience of self is the *self as object*...usually a bad, unwanted, or deficient object, though in some cases an overly idealized one—rather than the *self as agentic subject*...As a result of this...invalidation of one's primary experience by the internalized other, the sense of self *remains poorly articulated or distorted—usually both*—making it less of a resource for navigating the complexities of life.

(Chapter 1, "Living in an Airless World"; emphasis added)

The "usually both" refers to the fact that, on the one hand, the child's primary subjectivity, or potential self, has been largely unrecognized, un-mentalized, and under-responded to, creating the kinds of deficits in the senses of self and personal agency that Kohut wrote about. Yet, at the same time, these parents *were actively* perceiving and treating the child in toxically distorting, negating ways. Thus, the child's psychic reality was both *under-mentalized* and, if you will, *mis-mentalized*. It is this combination of traumas to the sense of self that led me to propose the twin processes of *deconstruction* and *re-subjectification* as ultimately both necessary in the treatment of serious airless world problems. This combination of traumas amounts to a circumscribed area of weakened or blocked development. Following Kohut, I believe that the selfobject dimension of the therapeutic relationship plays a key role in addressing this blockage; but it is a complex form of selfobject responsiveness that is called for—one that addresses not only the needs of the under-responded-to potential self but, just as crucially, the identificatory prison that continues to traumatize, control, and limit the patient's subjective world.

It would be helpful here to have a succinct clinical example. So, before returning to Martha I'm going to share a briefer vignette with a different patient that illustrates this more complex selfobject response.

Clint[1]

Clint was a patient in late middle age who spoke in articulate but very general ways about what he wanted in his life but had never achieved, and about his negative expectancies about what was possible for him in the future. It was easy for me to get almost hypnotically lulled into Clint's pessimism because of his lyrical eloquence and because the evidence of his life accomplishments to date seemed to support his gloomy predictions. He *had* failed in certain ways—failures that were understandable in light of his powerful, sadistic father's systematic efforts to undermine and crush his sense of competence and potency as an adolescent and young adult. It finally dawned on me that, while Clint's narrative had some basis in reality, he was, in fact, telling himself a story—a version of the story his father had told him about himself. This realization prompted me to say in a playful but serious way: *"I don't trust **any** generalizations you make about yourself or your future. I think we do better to stay with what is happening, and what you're feeling, **now**."* This became a kind of mantra for us for quite a while: one that always brought a knowing smile and a palpable sense of relief—relief that grew over time. It became part of the bulwark we were gradually constructing against the crushing power of the internalized voice of his father, and a marker of the potential space we were co-creating for the emergence of a new sense of self grounded in his own deeper belief about what was possible for him in what remained of his life. Of course, the mantra derived its power not only from its content but from its tone (knowing, playful, affectionate, supportive) and the fact that it came from me—a new kind of male authority figure who saw both Clint's potential and the forces he was battling in his efforts to actualize it.

I like this example for several reasons. This was not something I would have been able to say to Clint early in our work together. It took several years of listening to him, getting a sense both of how his life ambitions had become so derailed *and* of his strengths and potential strengths that were being perpetually strangulated by the internalized voice of his father, before I could formulate such a paradoxically simple but complex message. That message also grew out of our particular *ways of relating* to each other, which included the use of irony, humor, and a shared enjoyment of language, all in the context of a palpable mutual affection. Thus, it is a good example of the linked processes of specificity of recognition and connection in adult treatment.

What I would now add is that my being able to formulate and speak such a complexly supportive message represented the moment when our selfobject connection became more fully actualized. My statement, "I don't trust any generalizations you make about yourself or your future," said forcefully but playfully, is an example of *deconstruction*—it aimed to deconstruct the immobilizing, internalized narrative and voice of Clint's father, which at times reached psychotic proportions in the form of auditory hallucinations. I had been trying to do this all along in a more interpretive way but with little transformative effect. With the mantra, however, I became a stronger ally in Clint's heretofore *losing* battle with his father for control of his subjective reality. That forcefulness registered with him in a new way. I think here of some of George Atwood's (2012) forceful but supportive interventions with his psychotic patients. Clint's father had been a powerful figure, not just in the home but in the larger community. He was a captain-of-industry type from an era when such men were valorized for their success and power, with few constraints placed on their behavior. I was using my power, acquired in the first few years of our therapy, to insert a highly contoured psychic wedge between Clint and the ghost of his father. This all falls in the domain of the needed relationship—a uniquely evolved form of recognition and connection.

I suggest that, within the total needed relationship, Clint's experience of me as effectively defusing some of the power of that internalized voice registered as a necessary component of the selfobject experience set in motion by the mantra. This is a key point: *If we think of the selfobject transference as an expression of the patient's forward edge, for that transference to be fully actualized, the patient must experience the analyst as truly offering a path forward from where they are **now**, which means addressing the internalized impediments to self-actualization—the living sequelae of early relational trauma.* What marked my intervention with Clint as a selfobject experience was that whenever I would repeat the mantra or something like it, it opened up an *intersubjective pathway* between us—what I call *breathing together* (Stern, 2019a)—which simultaneously precipitated a state shift in him from his chronically beleaguered, defeated experience of himself and his life to a more positive, less encumbered, less shame-filled, more potent, and confident attitude toward what was possible for him going forward. As further evidence of this shift, I had known that throughout his adult life Clint had had the repeating nightmare that he was trapped underground beneath a sealed manhole. He could see light coming down around the edges, but with no possibility of escape. We understood that this image represented his fully sealed-off subjective self, which had been assaulted and strangulated by his father. Only with the introduction of the mantra did the dream shift: He was now pushing and pounding on the manhole cover from below, and it was slowly loosening and giving way, admitting more and more light, and air.

The other component of the mantra was the invitation to focus on, and take seriously, his here-and-now emotional experience as he interacted with his relational world—that is, the kind of therapeutic process we hope ultimately leads to what I call *re-subjectification*.

Now, Back to Martha

Even after ten years of analysis, Martha's airless world was still present in the form of her reflexive suppression of any intense affects and the resulting headaches that continued to occur in many sessions. To think about the kind of needed relationship and selfobject connection that have emerged in our work together, I need to give a fuller picture of who Martha is and how our relationship has evolved.

Having grown up in a cold, often cruel, almost totally negating family atmosphere, Martha alternated between *self*-deprecation and finding fault with *others*, often caustically and sadistically, when she felt frustrated with, or threatened by, the other in some way. I have referred to this kind of identification with the aggressor elsewhere, following Weiss, Sampson, et al. (1986), as "turning passive into active"—that is, doing to the other what was done to oneself (Stern, 2023). (See Chapter 4 for a delineation of "varieties of airlessness.") She did this with me as well, starting almost immediately. In our third session she reported the following dream: *We're walking together down a Maine country road. I'm new; she's showing me around. We come across some poor people. I give them money—it's the wrong thing, not what they wanted. She's disdainful.* Her association was to wonder if therapy with me was the right place for her.

As is often the case, the core themes of the treatment emerged in the first few sessions. I've never had a patient enter into an analytic process so quickly. Yet what emerged from her unconscious were suspicious, judgmental, disdainful reactions and feelings; questions about my sensitivity, competence, and boundaries; and hence questions about the safety of entering into a dependent relationship with me. One could sense that the attachment was almost immediate, like that of a neglected or abused child in desperate need of rescue and care. But it was not a case of love at first sight—on either of our parts. In Martha's world, people—especially those in authority—were presumed untrustworthy and potentially dangerous until proven otherwise.

During the first year, our relationship established itself as a productive, rapidly deepening analytic process in which Martha was bringing in more and more of her internal world and forming a selfobject connection and attachment to me that functioned increasingly as an emotional lifeline. Our session frequency increased from one to four meetings a week by the end of that year, each increase being transacted in a similar way. Whatever was happening in our sessions, positive or negative, Martha experienced any break as a frightening abandonment, leaving her alone in a state of anxious, angry non-existence. As a child she was always emotionally alone. But her parents, both successful academics, traveled frequently, seemingly heedless of the terrifying abandonment Martha felt as she and her brother were left in the care of often disengaged relatives. I was always the one who introduced the idea of adding another session, and she always reacted with a combination of (in her words) feeling both held and seduced. She expressed the fear that such further dependence and acknowledgment of my importance would lead to my taking advantage of her. But then we would work with her process around these anxieties, often expressed in dreams. When I proposed increasing to three times a week, she dreamed *she was imprisoned by the Nazis, but she escaped.* In a second dream: *I'm making some kind of pictorial lesson or interpretation, and she sees it's in the shape of a penis.* Her association was that I am a phallic man pushing something on her. But I'm also the holding parent who she can't wait to see at the next session. By the next session, she felt calmer about going ahead with three sessions a week. And so it went. I think Martha would say now that a critical element in these discussions was that we could talk about it all. Martha's experience of our being able to talk about everything was undoubtedly one of the factors contributing to the progressive development of our selfobject connection.

Over time, and I mean years, a kind of airlessness, or partial airlessness, came to pervade our transference-countertransference relationship. While there was always the selfobject lifeline and Martha's commitment to speaking honestly about what was on her mind, a tension took hold between *her* deep distrust and suspicion about my true feelings and expectations and *my* frustration at never seeming to make a difference in this basic distrust, no matter what I did or said. Adding to the tension was the anger I could always sense lurking near the surface with Martha—anger that could be triggered unpredictably by frustrations with me and the slowness of our process. All of this added up to a damned-if-I-did/damned-if-I-didn't quality in Martha's experience of me, and a wariness of the other on both of our parts.

If Martha experienced me in a given session as abandoning, distracted, judgmental, overly self-focused, controlling, or sadistic, these perceptions confirmed what she expected and feared (at the implicit relational level), causing her to feel less connected between sessions and come back angry. If, on the other hand, she experienced me as *with* her, understanding her, or being especially helpful, she would feel more connected, less alone, and typically more resilient between sessions. She would usually tell me this at the next session but was ambivalent about doing so, fearing it would feed my narcissism and/or provoke reciprocal feelings in me that could lead to my taking advantage of her. Thus, even in good times Martha remained suspicious of my true attitudes and motivations, which she assumed lay hidden behind my therapeutic façade. This limited the degree of relaxation and surrender she *or I* could allow, which in turn, I feared, was limiting the transformative potential of our work.

The main assumption she made about what lay behind my therapeutic persona was that I needed her to be a certain kind of good patient and that, if she relaxed her efforts to keep me gratified and engaged, I would quickly get bored, impatient, or angry, give up on her, and turn away. This seemingly unshakable assumption made her feel that she had to constantly be on guard and accommodate to my implicit requirements; and this vigilance played havoc with one of her primary goals for treatment: to be able to relax and be fully herself with me, without losing my interest and authentic therapeutic involvement. Adding insult to injury, Martha felt tremendous anger because of her accommodation to my *presumed* implicit conditions for working with her. This rage was represented in a highly aggressive, repetitive fantasy that she often had during sessions. In it she would get up and violently destroy everything in my office, except that she would not physically touch or harm me. This was similar to fantasies she had had as an adolescent of wanting to destroy all of her mother's valuable antiques, which filled their child-unfriendly home and which she felt her mother cared more about than she did about Martha. In short, in Martha's world one person's existence meant the other's erasure—an extreme version of Benjamin's (2004, 2018) doer/done-to dynamic.

For me, the most troubling effect of these undercurrents in our relationship was the constraints they placed on the development of feelings of mutual trust and analytic love. So long as there was no relief from the constant wariness, on both of our parts, of how we might be hurt or shamed by the other, conditions would not be safe for the development of mutual trust or love, limiting what was possible in the treatment. These tensions came to a head in an unpredictable, nonlinear way in a session in late 2015.

Martha, an accomplished professional journalist, began the session reporting that she had been reading a New York Times "Couch" column in which the author talked about how, in good treatment, the intermingling of two subjectivities becomes part of the patient's individual mind. She questioned whether that was happening for us. I asked her what was missing for her. "The warmth that would come from that," she said quickly. I acknowledged that the whole issue of coldness versus warmth and trust was crucial in our relationship but felt complicated. I said I thought we had a slowly evolving "emotional alchemy" in this regard. She seemed to get that, saying that on the coldness/warmth scale she was at about 4 or 5 out of 10 compared to the 1 she had started at. She then amended that to 3! I said: "That sounds about right!" She then asked directly about *my* emotional experience of *her*. I had to pause here and think carefully, sensing this was a "now moment" in the Boston Change Process Study Group's parlance (Stern et al., 1998). I reiterated that it was complex. I said I knew I felt a deep engagement with, and commitment to, her and a determination to speak the truth. I said: "That's a frame of potential warmth, but there's a lot to be held in that frame, including experiences of coldness, anger, and distrust." I said *she* doesn't have receptors for warmth, and *I* have needed to develop receptors that can tolerate and hold her coldness, anxiety, and anger. I added that this was a lot to digest, but she seemed to resonate with what I was saying!

She began the next day's session saying it was hard and scary for her to acknowledge that yesterday had been very meaningful and helpful, especially the idea of our developing a unique process with its own alchemy. She was afraid that in telling me she would be shamed, and it would be taken away. I wrote in my note that day that "I felt in a new and very good place with her in terms of my presence, affect receptivity, and attunement to her needs for a certain kind of analytic space." What's striking to me, as I review this session, is that putting words to my experience of our field changed the field for both of us. It provided a containing function for a force field that had felt in certain ways uncontained for years. My words somehow created more understanding, hope, and even warmth, in our connection, which affected how I, at least, was able to process things going forward.

This session marked a turning point in our treatment. What I said and how I said it seemed to reach Martha in a new way. So, the question is: What happened here? The first thing I would say is that, like my more cryptic intervention with Clint, this rather extended, somewhat complicated speech in response to Martha's questions was somehow well-fitted to her, and our shared, experience of our relationship up to that point (Sander's specificity of recognition and connection). In fact, I think this very specificity was part of what impressed her. It signified that I had been paying attention and processing our unique struggle with each other. My words and the way I expressed them had conveyed my genuine caring, my willingness to be honest about my own complicated feelings, and my sincere effort to make things work between us. Articulating the idea of an intersubjective field with its own evolving emotional alchemy created a connecting link between us that had been needed but had not yet existed as a nameable, mentalizable metaphor.

Importantly, this "moment of linking" had to take into account both of our subjective experiences of the other because that is precisely where the trouble lay—i.e., in our complex ambivalence toward each other, which we both sensed was limiting our connection. I had come to believe that Martha's and my particular needed relationship needed to make room for both of our subjectivities given that, in both her early relational and present internal worlds, one person's existence meant the other person's erasure—an extreme version of Benjamin's (2004) doer/done-to dynamic. Thus, I felt it was imperative not to erase my own subjectivity at the same time that I was empathically attending to Martha's subjective experience. I should say that for years Martha hadn't loved this approach. She had made clear her preference that I be "only empathic" and deal with my subjectivity on my own! In recent years, however, she has changed her mind, now feeling that it has been very important and helpful to her on the relatively rare occasions when I have directly shared something of my reactive emotional subjectivity.

The idea of an evolving, transforming field within a dedicated analytic frame of potential warmth was both relieving and freeing because it allowed us to have our real feelings in a way that freed them to evolve in the direction of greater connectedness. One might say, following Tolpin (2002), that my words relocated our seeming stuckness within a forward edge relational process. In the language of selfobjects, my rather complex intervention with Martha marked the beginning of a fuller, more complex selfobject connection between us. In short, our exchange opened a new pathway for the exchange of needed psychic air—a new experience of *breathing together*. Moreover, the selfobject experience went both ways: First, Martha felt my expressed understanding and presence during this exchange as a complex selfobject experience; then, hearing how meaningful it had been to her was a new selfobject experience for me *with* her. Our interchange in this session marked the beginning of a palpable, though of course not total, change in the ways Martha and I experienced each other, related to each other, and experienced ourselves with each other. New air was simultaneously entering both *our* intersubjective, and *Martha's* intrapsychic, worlds.

Fast forward to the present. In the intervening years, much has changed between Martha and me—really the whole tenor of our relationship. There have been other pivotal moments and interventions that have contributed to a deepening trust and relaxation with each other. Martha feels progressively stronger and, in her words, like she is starting to "exist" for the first time in her life; and this nascent sense of self is showing up in many contexts in different ways. As part of this transformation, my countertransference has shifted dramatically. I no longer approach our sessions with tense apprehension; I feel more confident about my ability to respond to almost anything Martha presents; and feelings of genuine enjoyment, liking, and (yes) love are naturally emerging and evolving in me. Yet there is still the problem of her headaches and the fact that she cannot let herself cry with me, even when she feels like it.

Here is a recent session in which all of this came fully into our process. After more than a year of remote therapy during the COVID-19 pandemic, we started to meet in person twice a week and by phone for the other two sessions. Martha vastly preferred being in person on my couch because of the more visceral holding environment it created, so the pandemic had been tough on her. This was a Monday phone session. That week we were meeting only on Monday and Tuesday, after which she was going on a one-week vacation.

She begins the session by saying she's having feelings of sadness at the impending separation—intense feelings. "I know I'll be fine," she reassures both of us. It has been years since the time when breaks of any length were extremely difficult for her. She now feels much stronger and able to hold me in mind as a real presence during our breaks.

I ask her to go into the feelings and say more. "There are strong feelings of sadness…I'm starting to feel tearful." Then she shares an image of running and jumping into my lap. She has had such images more often in recent years. I understand them as expressions of a needed therapeutic regression—signifying that she feels safer with me than she ever had with her parents.

"It's not sexual," she avows. "But this is ridiculous," she starts to say, and before she can say any more, I interrupt her and say firmly, "Stop, don't go there! That's your mother's voice."

"But this is from when I was a toddler. I'm not a toddler anymore." I say, "These feelings are real—they've been there ever since you *were* a toddler, and you were forced to shut them down."

"Yeah, I learned to dissociate them so I could function."

"I agree, but dissociating them didn't get rid of them. They never went away because they were never received by anyone, until now with me. These feelings and all the feelings from before and after."

"I think my mother didn't like my crying as a baby."

"That's probably right, so let's try to stay with it now because it's the only way to reclaim those feelings and needs."

"Now I'm having an image of me as a baby—it's a merger image. I'm lying on your body."

"Yes, your feelings and those needs go all the way back to that time."

"But you're going to get sick of me..." Again, I cut her off: "Stop it! These feelings are so important, just like the angry feelings you got in touch with in my office a few years ago. I really want to hear them fully—whatever's there."

(Pause)…"I'm feeling the sadness—I'm closer to tears than I can remember being in here."

"This is your core trauma and I want you to bring it in fully."

(Pause)…"This is what I always wanted from my mother, but that could never happen."

"Yes, there's real grief about that."

"I think I kept hoping I could do this with her—right up until she died."

"I know—that's because it was a real need—you needed that from her."

At the end she says, "I'm feeling a headache, but not as bad as usual…"

How to unpack what's happening here? First, there's a forward edge push within Martha to reclaim her own long-dissociated feelings and needs, and connect with me at the different developmental levels at which the original traumas occurred. I should say, parenthetically, that the fantasies of connecting with me, usually in some bodily way, have ranged from early childhood images, like those emerging here, to adult and young adult playful and sexual images, including, at an earlier stage in our work, perverse scenarios, which I also understood as forward edge efforts to master developmental traumas and derailments. Almost always, these images are shared with much shame and fear of my reaction. I have always tried to respond with total encouragement, reframing them as her efforts to go back and, in a sense, re-live these developmental breakdowns under better relational conditions. This would certainly be part of what I call re-subjectification.

It has been important to this kind of work that Martha not feel I am *too* invested in her being able to take these risks with me. She worries, for example, that I may be too narcissistically invested in whether or not she can cry in session. I have tried to reassure her that this is not the case: I don't need her to cry; maybe she will and maybe she won't before she ends therapy. But I also say that it seems to be something *she* feels is very important to her own sense of being able to fully relax and surrender in our relationship.

The thing I did that was new in this session—and who knows why I was moved to do it now for the first time in more than a decade of work—was to forcefully stop her when she started to second-guess her childlike images, longings, and feelings. That was totally spontaneous—and over the phone, no less!—but obviously heartfelt and emphatic. In the language of complexity theory (e.g., Galatzer-Levy, 2002), it was *emergent* from the total complexity of our relationship as it had been evolving for over a decade. In a way not dissimilar to what I did with Clint, I was inserting a contoured wedge between Martha and her mother's voice, effectively blocking it and inviting her to go for it and say whatever was there. This would be a good example of deconstruction-in-action—deconstructing the identificatory prison of her internalized mother's shaming, controlling ridicule. It is also an example of combining deconstruction and re-subjectification in the same intervention: simultaneously *clearing the way for*, and *inviting*, full expression of her unruly emotional subjectivity. And it seemed to work. She went further than she had before in allowing herself to own her earliest thwarted needs and longings, and her desperate efforts throughout her life to get her mother to respond to her more lovingly. And lo and behold, by the end of the session she could feel a deepening sadness with less of a headache!

This example also demonstrates how the processes of deconstruction and re-subjectification need to be emergent as fitted interventions within the context of the total needed relationship as it accrues greater specificity and complexity over time. I hope it also makes sense that, while Martha established a preliminary selfobject transference and connection with me almost immediately, the fuller selfobject connection—our experience of *breathing together*—could only develop within our unique needed relationship as it evolved nonlinearly and fitfully for over a decade. Finally,

I hope it is clear that, while I generally approach my work with Martha with a conscious intention to achieve progressive specificity of recognition and connection, in both of the dramatic sessions I have shared from her treatment the key interventions were more spontaneous and *emergent* than consciously thought out and intentional, suggesting a nonlinear, unconscious dimension to our collaboration and some of our most transformative interactions.

Note

1   I used the first part of this same case vignette in the final chapter of my book on needed relationships, but to illustrate a different set of ideas. I also used it briefly in my reply to Dan Shaw's discussion of my "Airless Worlds" paper in *Psychoanalytic Dialogues* (Stern, 2019b, p. 475). Finally, note that this is the same Clint I presented more briefly in the Introduction to this book as an example of airless world dynamics.

References

Atwood, G.E. (2012). *The abyss of madness.* New York, NY and London: Routledge.

Benjamin, J. (1990). Recognition and destruction: An outline of intersubjectivity. *Psychoanalytic Psychology, 7*(Suppl.): 33–47.

Benjamin, J. (2002). The rhythm of recognition: Comments on the work of Louis Sander. *Psychoanalytic Dialogues, 12*: 43–54.

Benjamin, J. (2004). Beyond doer and done to: An intersubjective view of thirdness. *Psychoanalytic Quarterly, 73*: 5–46.

Benjamin, J. (2018). *Beyond doer and done to: Recognition theory, intersubjectivity and the third.* New York, NY and London: Routledge.

Coburn, W.J. (2014). *Psychoanalytic complexity: Clinical attitudes for therapeutic change.* New York, NY and London: Routledge.

Galatzer-Levy, R. (2002). Emergence. *Psychoanalytic Inquiry, 22*: 708–727.

Galatzer-Levy, R. (2017). *Nonlinear psychoanalysis: Notes from forty years of chaos and complexity theory.* London and New York, NY: Routledge.

Harris, A. (2005). *Gender as soft assembly.* Hillsdale, NJ: The Analytic Press.

Hoffman, I.Z. (1998). *Ritual and spontaneity in the psychoanalytic process: A dialectical-constructivist view.* Hillsdale, NJ: The Analytic Press.

Kohut, H. (1971). *The analysis of the self: A systematic approach to the psychoanalytic treatment of narcissistic personality disorders.* New York, NY: International Universities Press.

Kohut, H. (1977). *The restoration of the self.* New York, NY: International Universities Press.

Marks-Tarlow, T. (2008). *Psyche's veil: Psychotherapy, fractals and complexity.* London and New York, NY: Routledge.

McKay, R. (2019). Bread and roses: Empathy and Recognition. *Psychoanalytic Dialogues*, *29*: 75–91.

Sander, L. (2008). *Living systems, evolving consciousness, and the emerging person: A selection of papers from the life work of Louis Sander* (G. Amadei & I. Bianchi, Eds.). New York, NY and London: Routledge.

Stern, D.N., Sander, L.W., Nahum, J.P., Harrison, A.M., Lyons-Ruth, K., Morgan, A.C., Bruschweiler-Stern, N., & Tronick, E.Z. (1998). Non-interpretive mechanisms in psychoanalytic therapy: The "something more" than interpretation. *International Journal of Psychoanalysis*, *79*: 903–921.

Stern, S. (2017). *Needed relationships and psychoanalytic healing: A holistic relational perspective on the therapeutic process.* New York, NY and London: Routledge.

Stern, S. (2019a). Airless worlds: The traumatic sequelae of identification with parental negation. *Psychoanalytic Dialogues*, *29*: 435–450.

Stern, S. (2019b). Breathing together: Reply to Harris and Shaw. *Psychoanalytic Dialogues*: 470-476.

Stern, S. (2023). Airless worlds and couples therapy. *Psychoanalysis, Self and Context*, *18*: 164–189.

Stolorow, R.D. (1997). Dynamic, dyadic, intersubjective systems: An evolving paradigm for psychoanalysis. *Psychoanalytic Psychology*, *14*: 337–364.

Stolorow, R.D., & Atwood, G.E. (1992). *Contexts of being.* Hillsdale, NJ: The Analytic Press.

Stolorow, R.D., Brandchaft, B., & Atwood, G.E. (1987). *Psychoanalytic treatment: An intersubjective approach.* Hillsdale, NJ: The Analytic Press.

Strozier, C.B., Pinteris, K., Kelley, K., & Cher, D. (2022). *The new world of self: Heinz Kohut's transformation of psychoanalysis and psychotherapy.* New York, NY: Oxford University Press.

Togashi, K., & Kottler, A. (2015). *Kohut's twinship across cultures: The psychology of being human.* London and New York, NY: Routledge.

Tolpin, M. (2002). Doing psychoanalysis of normal development: Forward edge transferences. *Progress in Self Psychology*, *18*: 167–190.

Weiss, J., Sampson, H., & The Mount Zion Psychotherapy Research Group. (1986). *The psychoanalytic process: Theory, clinical observations and empirical research.* New York, NY: Guildford Press.

Winnicott, D.W. (1962). The aims of psycho-analytic treatment. In D.W. Winnicott (Ed.), *The maturational processes and the facilitating environment* (pp. 166–178). New York, NY: International Universities Press.

Winnicott, D.W. (1965). *The maturational processes and the facilitating environment.* New York, NY: International Universities Press.

Chapter 3

Breathing Together
Complex Selfobjects and Therapeutic Action

In this chapter, I continue to look closely at the clinical processes through which intersubjective psychic air can be introduced into a patient's relatively airless intrapsychic world, focusing especially on the idea of "breathing together." As referenced in previous chapters, Kohut (1977) likened the psychological need for empathic resonance (and, by implication, selfobject relations) to the physical need for oxygen. I agree, as my work on airless worlds attests. But I have come to believe that the restarting of psychic breathing in developmentally traumatized patients requires what I call, metaphorically, *breathing together*—a complex intersubjective achievement that becomes possible only as the therapist comes to know and meet the patient in progressively fitted ways, while the patient is learning to know and connect with the therapist within the context of their uniquely co-created analytic frame and process. Examples of breathing together occurred with both patients in Chapter 2—Clint and Martha—at the very points where I wrote that a complex selfobject experience was emerging. I described it as *an intersubjective pathway* opening up between patient and analyst at an unconscious as well as a conscious level.

Breathing together is a form of relationality that emerges fitfully and nonlinearly over time and across many interactions and kinds of interaction. Early relational trauma transforms a patient's original potential self into an entire personal scheme for managing that trauma and adapting to the requirements and threats posed by the traumatizing but needed other(s). Thus, it makes sense that that patient will need *a relationship of a certain kind* to fully engage and transform that limiting, trauma-based, personal/relational scheme. Most critically, the patient needs to feel that the therapist *gets it*—that they grasp the vicissitudes of the patient's traumatized states, the historical and real-time conditions that gave and give rise to them, and

DOI: 10.4324/9781003585237-4

the adaptive personal scheme the patient has evolved for coping with the original traumas and their aftereffects. But beyond that, the patient also needs to feel that the therapist is *engaging with* them in ways they experience as *different* from the original traumatizing figure(s), and as *addressing* the patient's complex state of the moment so as to transform it in the direction of greater self-integrity, connectedness, trust, and capacity for psychic breathing in relation to the internalized, suffocating conditions of the past. In Sander's (2008) language, it is only through progressive specificity of both recognition and connection that full breathability becomes possible. This is never a smooth path: All manner of impasse may arise—some prolonged and seemingly insurmountable—on the path to a more trusting connection, full "useability" (Winnicott, 1969; Newman et al., 1988), and breathability. Indeed, it is the therapist's capacity to weather such turbulence and emerge in a place of greater recognition and connection that may be most compelling to the patient over time.

The following clinical narrative is presented in two parts; it tracks the nonlinear emergence of such a process with a patient who presented with "impossible" attachment conundrums.

Philip

Part 1

My first impression of Philip—a 50-ish, British-born, American-trained physician with a growing rural practice—was of a man who, at 6'2" with lanky good looks, was at once imposing and retiring, intelligent yet deferential, successful but nervous and unsure of himself. Beginning in our first session, there was an almost immediate feeling of mutual recognition and rapport. We connected quickly around my recognition of the nature of his struggles and his recognition that, for the first time, he was with someone who seemed to get him—his history and his agonies. This was especially compelling to Philip since, after numerous attempts at therapy, he had all but given up hope that he would ever emerge from his life-long sense of not being fully real or alive. The pain and urgency of his growing despair were violently expressed in his impulse to buy a gun and shoot himself in the head—a fantasy triggered every day as he drove past the gun shop on his way to and from his rural office. The immediacy of our mutual recognition under such despairing conditions is heady stuff for both patient and therapist. Could I actually become the lifeline Philip needed and had been implicitly searching for?

He opened our second session announcing that he felt "in turmoil." He felt "enticed by the prospect of working [with me]," but, at the same time, "overwhelmed by the sense of there being a lot of work to do." He was in touch with a feeling of "lack" and of being "too needy." He sensed he needed analysis but knew he would be afraid to "surrender" to it. "What if it doesn't help that much?" he worried—the experience he had had in all previous therapies.

I learned that Philip had been divorced for two years following a 20-year marriage. For the past year, he had been involved in an on-again, off-again relationship with Erin, a woman he had met in the waiting room of the therapist both were seeing at the time! As Philip was beginning to tell his story, I could see his experience of himself was largely defined by the cumulative registrations of him by his significant others—a central feature of airless world syndrome (see Chapter 1). For example, on one hand Philip felt enlivened when he was with Erin—feeling she saw things in him that had never been recognized before, thus potentially giving him a new lease on life. On the other hand, Erin's own history of traumatic loss predisposed her to needing Philip to make an immediate, full, unshakable commitment to her, and caused her to become enraged with his tendency to withdraw following any advance in their intimacy. She tended to pathologize his ambivalent cycling while at the same time exhorting him to do better. This left him feeling inadequate and guilty: afraid that if he did not accede to her requirements his hopes for greater self-actualization would be foreclosed, but panicked that, if he complied, he would completely lose his sense of self.

As this second session was concluding, I found myself joking with him about Erin's impatience. I said: *Just tell her: "We met in a therapist's waiting room, so it shouldn't be surprising that I need more therapy!"* Though you had to have been there, my saying this cracked up first Philip, then me, prompting an extended, uncontrolled laughing fit that clearly felt good to both of us. Where did this joke come from? I use humor a fair amount with patients, but rarely have I taken such an impromptu risk so early. I'm sure I was influenced by Jackie Gotthold's important work in the area of playfulness in psychotherapy (e.g., 2007). In hindsight, the joke represented a complex moment not just of meeting (Stern et al., 1998) but of becoming. In effect, it was saying that I saw how he projected both power and superior wisdom onto the woman, how he experienced himself as needing to comply with, and internalize, her framing of the situation and his character, and how his only way to preserve any semblance of an agentic self was to withdraw and reject the woman. At the same time, it suggested that there might be a voice in which he could assert his reality outside of a doer/done-to complementarity (Benjamin, 2018); all with the implication that I sensed in him greater strength, reflective capacity, and, as Winnicott would say, capacity to play, than he sensed in himself. But, perhaps more salient than any of these, it was a lived moment of intimacy and surprising familiarity. Following this session, Philip felt more emboldened with Erin and was able to express more directly his wish to slow their process down. Erin, unfortunately, could not relinquish her need to control things, so things blew up. Philip ultimately was able to end the relationship, though not without considerable guilt about letting her down, which was a replay of his life-long dynamic with his mother.

In short, this unpremeditated joke at the end of our second session emerged from an intersubjective potential space of recognition and connection that was rapidly accruing complexity and power at the implicit level. Moreover, the joke itself opened up new potential space—a new channel of humor and laughter—that would grow in importance and complexity as our relationship evolved. It also undoubtedly contributed to the early selfobject transference, which was rapidly evolving and becoming more complex.

Not until our third session did Philip reveal that he had a job offer in another city, which I will call Altville, to join the clinical faculty at the prestigious medical center where he had trained decades earlier. The job had the advantage of being more academic than his solo, rural practice; it would give him a clearer identity, automatic status, peers, and a sense of safety since he was familiar with both the institution and Altville's urban culture. The promise of Altville stood in stark contrast to Bleakville—the colder, more isolated region where he and I lived and worked. Moreover, he now revealed that he had a long-term relationship in Altville with a female colleague, Jenna. He had fallen for her when they were both medical students, but she was married at the time. However, they both ended up going through divorces and he had reached out to her for support in the middle of his. So now the opportunity was there to pursue the relationship more fully. And pursue it he did! They developed a serious romantic relationship during the same period when he was developing his analytic relationship with me.

Philip returned the next session worried he had "hurt" me by pitting Altville against psychoanalysis. He then revealed that he had a firm time frame within which he needed to respond to the Altville offer. At this point my head was starting to spin. It had felt like there was an authentic deepening of our analytic connection; but now it seemed like everything else in his life pointed toward Altville. Trying to get my bearings, *I said that common sense would suggest that he needed to figure out his life first, then figure out therapy. There were analysts in Altville too, and there was the possibility of his working remotely with me.* After a long pause he responded by saying he had been feeling better, more peaceful, since starting our sessions; he feels I help him feel his "real self." I heard this as evidence of a nascent selfobject connection.

He came in the following Monday saying, "I took the job," then spent the rest of the session expressing remorse, ambivalence, and embarrassment. He stated that the job "will only prop me up," but I couldn't tell if he believed this or was saying it to keep me engaged and hopeful that he would change his mind. By the next session he was saying "This [meaning in-person analysis] is what I need to do." All of this caused me to take a giant step back from the feeling of "all systems go" that had been developing in our first few sessions. Bollas (1987) wrote that "patients create atmospheres." I realized that Philip was creating a unique atmosphere with me, and I needed to pause to process what he was doing, what it meant, and what he might need from me. My first realization, a kind of interpretation to myself, was (as I wrote in my note that day): *"I can't need anything from him."* In particular, I couldn't need this potential analytic patient, whom I was growing to like, to choose to remain in treatment with me. It was already becoming clear that part of the needed relationship would be his having the freedom to be divided, indecisive, inconsistent, and even inconvenient without suffering undue resentment or impatience from me, as he had with Erin. This realization proved to be foundational during the first year of our work, as Philip increased to five sessions a week while keeping the Altville option open in a way that left me truly uncertain about what he would do.

I need to interrupt the clinical narrative briefly here to say something about the primary trauma of Philip's early life. Philip's mother emerged as the saddest example in my experience of what André Green (1975) had famously called "the dead mother complex." Initially characterizing her as "depressed and weak," Philip explained that both of his mother's parents had died very early—her father when she was two and her mother at nine, after which she was shuffled around among "uncaring aunts." While details of her early life remain obscure, the result was a deadened or shattered self, such that she was incapable of any sort of alive maternal interest or engagement and had been impervious to Philip's desperate efforts, from his earliest memories to the present day, to engage her in some form of responsiveness to his emotional needs. Rather, she had implicitly looked to him to take care of her and had a way of making him feel guilty for the sin of living his own independent life.

Returning to Philip and me, as things progressed it became evident that a major source of Philip's swings back and forth about committing to the analysis was his fear that I could not be counted on to be there for him in the long run. This was related to his feeling that he did not have what it takes to be a real analytic patient. He felt he lacked a self, such that he would have nothing to talk about, and I would only be subjected to his messy, irritable, needy, boring presence, and would inevitably withdraw. He knew that something about our connection was affecting his ability to sense himself and feel more real. But he had no faith that this would hold up over time. Here *I interpreted that he was starting to trust me but didn't trust these trusting feelings and was wary of making a major, life-altering decision based on them.*

We also came to understand that his fantasies about life in Altville were part of a life-long pattern of feeling that the only way to assure viability was to have a backup plan—some new place to go to that would support, and advance, his professional, financial, and social ambitions so that he would have at least the semblance of a life, even if he didn't have a real life. This basic strategy was so wired into his adaptive character organization that the thought of giving it up and committing to analysis with me in Bleakville filled him with panic. It seemed like too big a bet based on too little data. Yet, as the analysis was deepening and beginning to offer needed recognition and existential support, he found himself in the position of feeling anticipatory loss and panic, either way he might choose.

Living inside this atmosphere of seemingly impossible attachment conundrums began to cause a form of "relational strain" (Stern, 2014). Philip's child self needed me not only to hang in there with him through all his opposing impulses and movements, but to become increasingly invested and attached, even as his adult self needed to preserve the right to bolt at any moment. And in fact, I *was* becoming more attached, which, inevitably, activated my own history and struggle with attachment insecurity. Somehow, with the help of Bion's (1970) idea of "negative capability," and my acceptance of the inescapable vulnerability of my situation with Philip, I was able to make a shift into a place of relative, though far from total, comfort with the uncertainty. (Bion had taken the concept of negative capability from the poet John Keats who, in 1817, had defined it as "when a man is capable of being in uncertainties, mysteries, doubts, without any irritable reaching after fact or reason.") In retrospect, I see this as a theoretically informed emergence of fittedness made possible by progressive transformations in my experiential states toward increasing complexity and inclusiveness of Philip's conflicting self-states. While these transformations did not make me immune to countertransference reactivity, they did free me to be able progressively to observe and comment on Philip's effect on me and our process as "analytic objects" (Green 1975; Ogden, 1994).

For example, a sequence that took place over several sessions began with my interpreting that *to the extent that he felt he had to manage everyone in order to keep both of his options open, he must feel alone in a certain sense*. He responded by saying he felt he was betraying me, at which point I invited him to say more. He then said he felt there was a destructive, spiteful part of him that felt I really couldn't help him and had been too confidently optimistic about what was possible. I was "kindly," he said, but was not reckoning with how depressing his life in Bleakville was. *I encouraged him to give voice to these spiteful feelings*. Without hesitating, he said he felt defiant, destructive, and like he wanted to have a tantrum, but just as quickly, he shifted to feeling "guilty, ashamed, and unappreciative."

He began the next session saying he was "hardening" in his decision to sign the contract and move to Altville. This shocked me, though it shouldn't have. The word that came into my mind as I sat with it was "violence." Something about this announcement felt like an act of violence. Feeling angry and confused, I chose to say little throughout the rest of the session, waiting to see how things would play out. Philip's halting monologue was mainly self-excoriating, professing shame and embarrassment at his behavior. After the session, which was my last of the day, I found him waiting in the stairwell of my building. He quickly moved toward the front entrance and held the door for me as I walked out, looking at me with despair and urgency. *I said (in a compassionate voice) that we would talk about it all in the morning*. The next day he said he was feeling suicidal, tortured by this choice he couldn't make. At that point *I shared my thought from the previous day that there was violence in his telling me he was hardening toward leaving—violence to us and to himself.* He resonated with this, revealing that he had been having very violent fantasies of self-evisceration—like "shooting myself in the stomach or the asshole and blowing myself apart." *I said that this was in part because there had been much emotional violence in the deprivations of his childhood, and some physical violence from his alcoholic father.*

I would describe this whole sequence as a form of breathing together in the crunch (Russell, 2006). When I invited Philip to give voice to his spiteful, angry feelings he ultimately expressed them in an understated British way when he announced that he was "hardening" in his decision to sign the contract and move to Altville. His use of the word hardening came as a shock, at which point I shut down and gave myself space to process it. This enabled me, through a kind of reverie, to quickly get in touch with and name the violence he was doing both to himself and our relationship. Naming this to myself allowed *me* to "breathe" more freely. Naming it out loud the next day freed *him* to fully reveal the violence of his suicidal fantasies, suggesting that an *unconscious pathway* had opened up between us. All of this accrued to a deepening of the needed relationship and our selfobject connection.

This phase reached a crescendo when Philip actually signed the contract to take the Altville position… Then, over the next few weeks, he walked it back, finding legal reasons to withdraw, given that they had reduced some of the important benefits he had been promised. With this act he had burned his bridges to Altville, at least for the time being, thus ushering in a new phase of dealing with the commitment he was now making to remain in Bleakville with me.

Predictably, this prompted the side of his panic having to do with his dependency on someone he could not yet fully trust. He entered a weeks-long paralyzed, shutdown state, claiming that he didn't know what to talk about—like there was nothing there except emptiness and frustration with himself. One could sense his empty, deadened mother in the background. I understood that this was the very state he equated with his true underlying, deficient self—the state he was certain would ultimately drive me away. There were sessions when I said little, and I *could* find myself drifting away—in what I sensed even then were micro-enactments. *I knew, and interpreted to Philip, that whatever this was, it was not the "nothing" he feared it was. Rather, it was a "something"—a something he needed me to live through and not turn away from.* As he saw that I wasn't going anywhere, there was a gradual process, right out of Winnicott (1960/1965), of his relinquishing his "caretaker self" that had brought him to analysis, leaving his truer, very young, needful self in my hands, accompanied by a progressive sense of relaxation, hope, vitality, and, in moments, even euphoria. Of course, reversals continued, but in a more contained, less existentially threatening way.

Conclusion to Part 1

This first phase of Philip's and my work together dramatizes the evolution and co-creation of a needed relationship with progressive specificity of both recognition and connection. The therapeutic yield of this relational process was the emergence of an increasingly full and complex selfobject connection, marked by state-shifts in Philip in the direction of greater realness, aliveness, and a kind of relaxation or peacefulness specific to his history of relational trauma and his unique and deepening relationship with me. As Philip and I underwent and survived his head-spinning ambivalence, my consciousness, presence, and *voice* were, in highly nonlinear ways, acquiring an increasingly complex fittedness or "with-ness" (Reis, 2011), enabling me to provide, and the two of us to co-create, the unique potential space he needed with me in order to gradually and more fully enter our relationship. We were slowly, fitfully, learning to breathe together.

Part 2

In this section I continue examining the evolution of the needed relationship in my work with Philip through the first year of the COVID-19 pandemic, during which the necessity of remote therapy seriously threatened our nascent psychoanalytic project.

During the year between Philip's decision to remain in Bleakville to pursue treatment with me and the onset of the pandemic, our five-times-a-week, on-the-couch analysis consolidated and became organized around certain core themes and struggles. Early in our work together he had asked about the possibility of seeing me five times a week. I could infer in a general way where this might be coming from, but during our first year of committed analysis he was able to name it. He sensed it was his "infant self," and sometimes his "toddler self," that he felt he was re-experiencing as the treatment deepened, and that that required the steady, in-person, visceral experience of feeling held as he lay on my couch, whether silently or verbally engaged.

Although his indecision between Altville and Bleakville didn't totally disappear, the main issue that now emerged was his uncertainty about whether I, and analysis, could provide the transformative experience he knew he needed in order to feel more alive and real. This felt to both of us like a high-stakes gamble, where failure would likely cause him to give up forever on finding another human being he could trust to help him in such a fundamental way.

During that year a pattern emerged that was not unlike the pattern of the first year where he went back and forth about Altville versus me and Bleakville. The new pattern was more analytically contained but could feel almost as threatening. There were frequent periods when he would feel stuck in a state of inner "bleakness," insubstantiality (which he referred to as "nothing" or "nothingness"), "doubt" or "disbelief" in me and the process, and hopelessness that things would ever really change. This state was typically marked by long silences and apparent withdrawal into himself. He would express extreme frustration with himself for not being able to say anything and felt certain that these prolonged states would cause me to withdraw and ultimately turn away. Though I knew I would not turn away, it was sometimes a struggle to stay focused on him, and I could begin to share his sense of hopelessness about what was possible.

But always, at some point, something would shift, and Philip would emerge into a state of greater aliveness, realness, optimism, and most importantly, belief in me and the fact that *he seemed to matter to me*. When his state changed, it felt very real and infectious; so my state, and what you might call the state of the relationship, also changed. There was the feeling that this more confident/connected/optimistic/alive state was the more real and that good things really were happening in the treatment. But, as with his earlier state shifts between leaning toward Altville and leaning toward analysis and Bleakville, where both states felt like the more real state when he was in them, the same was true of the new version of hope vs. hopelessness.

It was often, though not always, true that something he or I could ultimately identify was responsible for these state shifts in either direction. The most frequent cause was any break in our sessions, whether a long break or even our weekend breaks. When we were meeting daily in person both I and our relationship felt tangibly real to Philip, causing *him* to feel more real. But during breaks I became an "abstraction," and he would drift inexorably into a state of aloneness, non-existence, and despair. However, breaks were not the only causes of the negative state shifts. Thus, it became a regular part of what you might call my technique with Philip to wonder what may have happened between us to cause the shift. Most of the time he would draw a blank, feeling it was just something within him that caused the change. This served the purpose of taking me off the hook and reaffirming his life-long beliefs about himself. But when I persisted in my assumption that he was reacting to something real that I had either done or not done, and especially when I could identify some likely cause, he would admit that I was probably right, and things would quickly start to shift back to the other state. In fact, it was my persistence in identifying my role in these state shifts that impressed him as different than anything he had experienced growing up, and as signifying that maybe he, Philip the real person, mattered to me.

Enter COVID-19 in March 2020. The abrupt change to remote therapy put us, like everyone else, into a state of disorienting shock, such that the full implications did not register immediately. The first tangible threat to our relationship was the immediate and total shutdown of Philip's medical-surgical practice, given that his area of practice was not one of those deemed essential as the hospitals were filling up with COVID cases. He worried that, if his income completely dried up, he would no longer be able to afford our sessions. I reassured him that, if that really happened, "we would figure something out." My spontaneous offer turned out to be very meaningful: He said his parents would never have been there for him in that way. Fortunately, the threat soon receded as he was able to resume work two or three days a week. Only then did the reality that we would not be meeting in person again for the foreseeable future begin to sink in.

As early as April 2020, Philip could say for the first time: "The phone works better than I might have thought, but it's not like in person. My infant self has lost something. I don't feel as held." The choice of phone over video was Philip's, though we both thought phone might feel closer than video to being on the couch.

Not surprisingly, the loss of in-person sessions caused Philip to think again about moving to Altville. By then his relationship with Jenna, mentioned earlier, had matured into a fully committed romantic relationship, which, in itself, created tensions around his staying in Bleakville. Initially, Jenna had made clear her wish for him to be in Altville, and he could see the appeal of being there. But it also scared him because of his life-long anxiety, beginning with his mother, that to give himself over to a woman meant losing his self in the process. He sensed, or, really, knew, that he would need me and analysis to be able to make things work with Jenna. Thus, in a way, it was better for both of them for Philip to stay in Bleakville, at least for the time being. And amazingly, Jenna got that: She assured him that she was committed to their relationship either way he decided.

By late April, Philip was in a state of despondency around our reduced therapeutic connection. The constraints imposed by the pandemic engendered a pervasive sense of helplessness—the feeling that there was nothing to be done about a loss which carried dire consequences. I felt helpless along with him. I concurred that he needed in-person analysis, and I was feeling my own version of despair, or at least grave concern, about how and whether we could survive this blow to his potential well-being. During that session, my own worry and sense of helplessness caused me to just quietly stay with Philip's despondency and anger without seeing or offering any solution or brilliant perspective on it—something akin to Stolorow's (2014) "emotional dwelling" and Grossmark's (2016) "companioning." And it seemed to help. At the end of that session he said he didn't feel totally alone in his despair. In the next session he could say that talking by phone *about* the limits of phone therapy made a difference in his feeling of connection, potential, and hope. "It's amazing what happens!" he exclaimed.

You can see from this discovery that I, and Philip and I together, would be grappling with the relative importance of two meanings of the word *presence*. To what degree did Philip's experience of getting what he needed from our relationship depend on what Russell (2006) calls "embodied co-presence" (i.e., our bodies being in the same room); and to what degree did my recognition of, and attuned presence with, Philip through the phone provide enough connection for him to feel that both he and I were real, or at least real enough? If I say the clear answer to this two-part question is "yes," that begins to capture the complexity of the needed relationship he and I were co-creating in response to COVID. As often happened, by the next session his sense of amazement about what had been possible by phone was eclipsed by his again "feeling less held by remote therapy and less reassured and appeased, more hollow." I wrote in my note that day: *How to hold the impossibility of being held?*

At around this time—early May 2020—the thought occurred to me that we had a back deck at our house that was potentially private and, in warm enough weather, could safely accommodate two people sitting face to face, six feet apart. Also, a patient could park in our driveway and walk across the back yard to the deck without having to enter the house. I brought this idea to the IAPSP Zoom pandemic support group that Heather Ferguson and I were co-leading, asking them if they saw any problems with my try-ing this with Philip. They were very enthusiastic but raised two main ques-tions: (1) How would Philip feel about coming to my home? And (2) would there really be sufficient privacy? At the time, which was the height of COVID, my wife and young adult daughter were also living and working in the house. But I worked it out with them (it was a tough negotiation!) that they would be upstairs on the second floor for the hour that a patient and I were on the deck. The privacy concerns settled, I floated the idea by Philip at our next session. His reaction was to feel "touched" that I would offer this and had given it so much thought. In his words, it somewhat lifted his despondency about feelings of "tenuousness" and the "incompleteness of his existence."

We had our first deck session on May 22. "It was a perfect, beautiful day," I wrote in my note.

> As soon as we were through the initial settling into our socially distant chairs, he turning slightly away and looking up at the trees, there was a sense of letting go into a calm, connected place. It was clear, being in per-son made a huge visceral difference in his sense of connection with me and with himself; and I would add, vice versa—I felt that too. Here on the deck, we didn't have to work so hard to "feel together" as we did on the phone.

As the session unfolded, I was aware that silences, in particular, felt differ-ent in person. They had a holding quality rather than the more blank quality one can feel on the phone. Sitting with me on the deck, Philip got in touch with powerful feelings of sadness, grief, and anger—grief at never having mattered in his family of origin the way being on my deck signified his mattering to me, and anger at all the wasted years before he found analysis. He said he could only feel these things with me. We agreed to do this once a week, weather permitting.

So, which was it? Was it Philip's being in person on my deck that made the difference and carried most of the therapeutic action, or was it the symbolic meaning of my having invited him to do it in the first place, signifying that he mattered to me? I have come to believe, as part of my general understanding of the therapeutic action of psychoanalysis, that patient and analyst, mostly unconsciously and using the tools at hand, stage *analogues* in the treatment relationship of the essential relational conditions that the patient had needed but not experienced in their family of origin. I view Philip's need to be in person as like a primary, irreducible, psycho-biological need—the necessary condition for what he called his "infant self" to feel sufficiently, viscerally connected and held. That this need was so totally and abruptly thwarted by the pandemic threw a major wrench into the treatment, posing a seemingly insurmountable obstacle for us to contend with.

In my book on needed relationships, I wrote about the *principle of necessity* as a primary driver of the analytic process (See Stern, 2017, Chapter 4)—necessity as in "Necessity is the mother of invention." I credit that principle with prompting the chain of thought that led to my inviting Philip to meet with me on our back deck. We couldn't meet every day, but we could meet once a week. We met every Friday, when the weather cooperated, from late May through early November. As the weather grew colder, however, requiring us to wear coats for the last month or so, Philip grew increasingly worried about the impending return of winter bleakness without the balm of in-person sessions.

By mid-December he was seriously missing our in-person meetings and feeling discouraged about it being so long before we could meet again in the same space. He reported the return of dreams in which he was doing violence to himself with a gun. At this point of seemingly impossible therapeutic roadblocks, the principle of necessity again kicked in, prompting me to ask Philip what he thought of the idea of coming to my house occasionally on a Friday and walking with me up and down the relatively quiet dirt road our house was on. It wouldn't be optimal for a therapy session, I said, but at least we would be in person. Appreciative of the invitation, he said he would think about it. By the next session he was "feeling more optimistic" because of my offer. *He said he felt like he' was searching for a home, and our relationship was becoming a kind of home for him.*

Our first walking session occurred on December 23. It was a nice day for walking—35 degrees, calm, warm afternoon light, with little traffic on the road. Clad in winter parkas, our rhythm of walking together took on a calm, meditative quality. Small talk gradually shifted to his speaking of feeling grateful for my doing this with him—again, like he mattered. But then he talked about his slippage into a darker place on the weekends, and his impatience with himself for still being so needy. I said I had a more positive take: Analysis is a slow process and his slippage during weekends was understandable, given that we were still at a relatively early stage in that process. In fact, I added, in my experience he was progressing rather quickly! "But of course," I added, "as a psychoanalyst I think in geological time!" All of this amounted to a new version of breathing together—a unique form of relational fittedness that contributed to the selfobject functioning of our evolving connection.

At first, I had agreed to walk only when the weather was relatively comfortable, like high 20s or above and not snowing. But this led to too many weeks in a row without meeting. So, necessity again intervened, causing me to change the policy to walking *every* Friday *except* when conditions were truly too harsh. By mid-January, Philip was clearly in a lighter, stronger place: He felt like something was "holding" better, even when we were not meeting. He added that "something transformational was happening incrementally." He wasn't getting as depressed. Following a weekend in late January when he had been in Altville with Jenna and had missed our Friday walk, he said he had missed meeting in person but felt present and alive through the weekend—things felt "firmer." He credited these changes to my having been "tenacious." Something was shifting in him toward greater "faith" and "belief."

By early 2021, when the first vaccines were proving effective against the Delta variant, I began to return to my office, first one day a week, then two, then three. Philip has continued to have oscillations—though far less extreme and prolonged—between periods when he feels bleak, insubstantial, and hopeless and those when he feels increasingly confident, buoyant, and like the analysis has been life-saving.

Conclusion to Part 2

Stepping back, if we use my rubric of the needed relationship to think about what happened between Philip and me during the first year of the pandemic, I would argue that the pandemic, and the forced shift to remote therapy, required dramatic changes in the surface structure of our needed relationship but not in the deep structure. Philip needed the in-person sessions on the back deck and our winter walks, but my offering these opportunities grew out of a more general analytic effort to continue meeting him in ways I sensed we needed in order to do our essential work. During our first two years he and I had, to use Winnicott's term, co-created a unique potential space for our developing analytic engagement—an engagement that was beginning to bear fruit in important ways. The pandemic radically altered the external conditions, and these changes necessitated a re-imagining and, so to speak, a "curving" of potential space to accommodate to the new reality while making possible the continuation of our essential work. One aspect of that curved space was meeting Philip on my back deck and on our winter walks. But equally important were the phone sessions when I silently stayed with his, and sometimes our, senses of despair and uncertainty about the limitations of remote therapy. It was these two kinds of experience in combination, within the larger context of our overall analytic process, that fitfully enabled our growing capacity to *breathe together* under adverse conditions, and underwrote Philip's progressive experience of me as a complex, transformational selfobject.

In retrospect, one fortuitous aspect of the pandemic was captured in Philip's word "tenacious," which he used to describe my determined efforts to try to meet with him in person frequently enough. This kind of tenacity might never have been necessary under ordinary pre-pandemic conditions. But, within the unique curvature of our potential space brought about by the pandemic, it came to signify to Philip that he must *really matter* to me in a way he had never experienced.

References

Benjamin, J. (2018). *Beyond doer and done to: Recognition theory, intersubjectivity and the third.* New York, NY: Routledge.

Bion, W.R. (1970). *Attention and interpretation.* London: Karnac.

Bollas, C. (1987). *Shadow of the object: Psychoanalysis of the unthought known.* New York, NY: Columbia University Press.

Gotthold, J.J. (2007). "Do you believe in magic?" Articulating a coconstructed dynamic systems approach to a child treatment: A discussion of Hilke's "Miss Nicht". *International Journal of Psychoanalytic Self Psychology 2*: 209–217.

Green, A. (1975). The analyst, symbolization, and absence in the analytic setting (On changes in analytic practice and analytic experience). *International Journal of Psycho-Analysis, 43*: 436–440.

Grossmark, R. (2016). Psychoanalytic companioning. *Psychoanalytic Dialogues, 26*(6): 698–712.

Keats, J. (1817/1952). Letter to George and Thomas Keats, 21 December, 1817. In M.B. Forman (Ed.), *Letters*. 4th edition. London: Oxford University Press.

Kohut, H. (1977). *The restoration of the self.* New York, NY: International Universities Press.

Newman, K.M., Kligerman, C., & Terman, D.M. (1988). Countertransference: Its role in facilitating the use of the object. *Annual of Psychoanalysis, 16*: 251–276.

Ogden, T.H. (1994). *Subjects of analysis.* Northvale, NJ: Jason Aronson.

Reis, B. (2011). *Silence and quiet: A phenomenology of wordlessness.* Panel presentation at the annual spring meeting of the American Psychological Association, Division 39, New York, NY.

Russell, P.L. (2006). The theory of the crunch. In R.L. Russell (Ed.), *Smith college studies in social work, volume 26* (pp. 9–21). Binghamton, NY: Haworth Press.

Sander, L. (2008). *Living systems, evolving consciousness, and the emerging person: A selection of papers from the life work of Louis Sander* (G. Amadei & I. Bianchi, Eds.). New York, NY and London: Routledge.

Stern, D.N., Sander, L.W., Nahum, J.P., Harrison, A.M., Lyons-Ruth, K., Morgan, A.C., Bruschweiler-Stern, N.,, & Tronick, E.Z. (1998). Non-interpretive mechanisms in psychoanalytic therapy: The "something more" than interpretation. *International Journal of Psychoanalysis, 79*: 903–921.

Stern, S. (2014). *Discussion of Joye Weiselbarth's "courting the real and stumbling in reality."* Presented at the annual meeting of the International Association of Psychoanalytic Self-Psychology, October, 2014.

Stern, S. (2017). *Needed relationships and psychoanalytic healing: A holistic relational perspective on the therapeutic process.* New York, NY: Routledge.

Stolorow, R.D. (2014). Undergoing the situation: Emotional dwelling is more than empathic understanding. *International Journal of Psychoanalytic Self Psychology, 9*: 80–83.

Winnicott, D.W. (1969/1971). The use of an object and relating through identifications. In D.W. Winnicott (Ed.), *Playing and reality* (pp. 86–94). London: Tavistock Publications.

Chapter 4

Airless Worlds and Couples Therapy

Some years ago, a couple was referred to me after the husband had been caught by his wife in the early months of an affair. As we dug into the couple's breakdown of constructive dialogue over many years it became clear that the husband had felt controlled, vilified, and rejected by the wife. Having had a cold and controlling mother from whom he had never fully separated internally, he experienced himself as being manipulatively controlled and rejected by his wife, with no effective means of standing up to her. Furthermore, like a child, he took on the wife's attributions as his own. If she saw him as a bad parent, he identified with that and, at least in part, came to see himself as a bad parent. The wife felt similarly devalued and criticized by the husband, as she had been by her critical, demanding mother, also with no effective means of addressing her feelings directly.

In retrospect, I would now describe this couple as living in an airless intersubjective world. The hallmark of the syndrome in couples is ongoing breakdowns of constructive dialogue, with no capacity to get space from or repair such breakdowns. As with individuals, airless world dynamics occur on a continuum of severity (pervasiveness) across different couples. It is at the extreme end, where there is virtually no capacity for constructive dialogue, that the metaphor is most apt and the model most helpful. But I have also found it useful with couples manifesting more circumscribed areas or forms of airlessness.

In what follows I illustrate the application of an airless world framework with couples by focusing on my treatment of the couple introduced above. First, however, I propose an expansion of the airless world paradigm to include some "varieties of airlessness" not covered in the original paper (Chapter 1), but which I find relevant to working with different couples, including the couple I will be focusing on. Next, I apply airless world

DOI: 10.4324/9781003585237-5

theory to working with couples at a conceptual level. Finally, I will share my process with the couple in question, highlighting specific interventions aimed at introducing needed psychic air into their airless system.

The airless world model primarily concerns *unconscious psychodynamic configurations* present in individuals and (as I argue here) in couples as well, rather than a particular technical approach with either individuals or couples. The model has technical implications, as will be demonstrated below, but it is primarily a model of the mind (or the dynamic interaction of two minds), and that dynamic understanding is generative of the particular technical approach that emerges in a given case. Extending the airless world paradigm to couples is consistent with my general approach to couples therapy, which emphasizes what I call *dialogue breakdown analysis* (Stern, 2013). Couples in serious couples therapy are, almost by definition, dealing with some form of dialogue breakdown, and I see it as the couple therapist's job to analyze the often complex forms such breakdowns can take and be able to help couples restore, or, as is often the case, help them develop for the first time, the capacity for dialogue around significant issues. One might say, metaphorically speaking, that the areas of dialogue breakdown in a given couple are like "pockets of airlessness" in that couple's overall communicative system. If those pockets expand to include all or most of a couple's communications, that couple is living in an airless intersubjective world.

Varieties of Airlessness: Common Denominators

Since writing the 2019 paper (Chapter 1), I have recognized that there are subtypes or varieties of airlessness, reflecting different kinds of trauma history. It is therefore useful (in treating both individuals and couples) to delineate these variations along with the common denominators that link them as airless world phenomena.

The Under-Responded-to Child

In Chapter 1 I focused on the trauma of parental negation and the consequent identification with negation that almost inevitably ensues. I alluded to the fact that "as a result of this...invalidation of one's early experience by the internalized other, the sense of self remains *poorly articulated or distorted—usually both*—making it less of a resource for navigating the complexities of life" (Chapter 1, "Living in an Airless World"; emphasis added). At the beginning of Chapter 3, I explained that with any form of debilitating parental negation there are two things going on at once: (1) The parent is *not seeing*, recognizing, attuning to, or supporting the child's true self (authentic feelings, needs, perceptions, gestures, states, developmental trajectories, etc.); the self is under-responded-to and as a result is weakened and remains underdeveloped. (2) At the same time, the parent is *systematically distorting* all of these aspects of the child's self in accord with the parent's pathogenic ways of experiencing and relating to the child. In other language, there is both a *failure of mentalization* (Fonagy et al., 2002) and a simultaneous experience of "*mis-mentalization*" by the parent(s).

In her discussion of my "Airless Worlds" paper in *Psychoanalytic Dialogues*, Adrienne Harris (2019) implied that these two elements do not always occur together. She expressed particular interest in a group of patients who were mainly unseen and under-responded-to by a relatively absent, self-absorbed, deadened, depressed, or otherwise neglecting parent, without the parent(s) coercively, narcissistically, imposing their own needs, values, distortions, and expectancies on the child. I would say that, in such cases, there is still an airless world—the child is not getting crucial recognition, responsiveness, and developmental support—but it has the characteristics of emptiness, non-existence, deadness, or pure aloneness rather than subjugation to a narcissistically controlling/distorting other. My patient Philip from Chapter 3 is an example of someone who grew up in this kind of airless world. There is now a literature that focuses on patients with this kind of trauma, beginning with André Green's famous (1983) paper, "The Dead Mother," and represented more recently in Anne Alvarez's (2012) work with what she calls "the undrawn patient." Amy Schwartz-Cooney, in her 2018 paper on "vitalizing enactment," describes a creative relational approach to working with such patients.

Chaotic Families

A second variation is the chaotic family in which one or both parents do not have the requisite inner structure and stability to provide good-enough, or at least reliable-enough, parenting. This was true in the wife's family of origin in the clinical example introduced above. Her mother had been seriously mentally ill (or at least diagnosed as such) when she was a child, with some prolonged hospitalizations. When home, the mother was erratic, disorganized, demanding, and critical. The wife, as a child, learned that she was basically on her own to take care of herself and was also enlisted in taking care of her mother in different ways. Not surprisingly, she became a psychiatrist. Some might recognize here the conditions for the development of disorganized attachment (e.g., Beebe & Lachmann, 2014; Wallin, 2007). I agree but have found that the attachment paradigm doesn't capture the airlessness of such patients' early intersubjective worlds (and consequent intrapsychic worlds). It misses the core complex of aloneness, the sense of being at the mercy of the powerful other, failure to separate, an inability to grieve the loss of what one never received, and a weak sense of personal agency in relational contexts (Stern, 2019).

* * *

In both the cases of the under-responded-to child and the child of a chaotic family, the negation of self is more implied than systematically imposed. The child is simply not seen or responded to in needed ways, thereby inducing intolerable aloneness, anxiety, and overwhelm, and implicitly communicating that the child either doesn't matter or does not really exist in the parent's mind.

Turning Passive into Active

My 2019 paper (Chapter 1) focused on the *introjective* version of identification with the aggressor (Ferenczi, 1933)—the form in which children learn to experience and treat *themselves* as they have been experienced and treated. But all clinicians know examples of the opposite version in which, "turning passive into active" (Weiss et al., 1986, p. 113), the child identifies with the parent's position in the relationship. Rather than (or in addition to) being locked in perpetual self-negation, the child learns to self-righteously negate, devalue, and even sadistically humiliate others in the style of the parent(s). Both the passive and active forms of identification with the aggressor have an underlying paranoid element, which can play out in individual therapy, but also in couples therapy. This was the case with my patient Martha in Chapter 2 and, as you will learn shortly, with the husband of the couple I will be focusing on in this chapter. Both the passive and active forms of identification with the aggressor can exist side-by-side, or in alternation, in the same person. The common denominator is that both types represent controlling forms of identification with a negating parent from which the subject has established little space or "air."

Every Airless World is Unique

Readers undoubtedly have encountered their own airless world variations with different patients and couples. Identifying different types of airless world is helpful in locating a given patient or couple in relation to certain psychodynamic dimensions. But when it comes down to it, each person, or couple, suffering from some form of this syndrome is experiencing a unique airless world with unique features and complexities that require prolonged empathic immersion and effort by the therapist to apprehend, comprehend, and meet in ways that begin to introduce needed psychic air. This empathic task is of course more complex with couples where there are two individual airless worlds to comprehend, the uniquely co-created airless world of the couple's relationship, and, inevitably at times, the airless world that can develop within the therapeutic system.

Common Elements

Each of the foregoing variations has its own distinct features, but they share the following characteristics that make them airless world phenomena: (1) a profound underlying sense of aloneness; (2) a failure to evolve healthy senses of self and personal agency; (3) a consequent failure in separation-individuation (Mahler, Pine, & Bergman, 1975), and hence a persistent dependency on the needed other; (4) an inability to grieve the loss of that which one has needed but never received; and (5) a tendency to unconsciously identify with the other's negating perspective. All these features can lead to deficits in the capacity for the kinds of dialogue needed in healthy-enough partnered relationships.

Intersubjective Airless Worlds in Couples

Understanding the nature of airless world phenomena in individuals is useful for recognizing how such dynamics play out in coupled relationships. As one gets to know patients (and couples) with airless world issues, a frequent common feature is the absence of true dialogical or intersubjective relating in their early family histories: The parents were not, for the most part, capable of recognizing and mentalizing their child's subjective experience and needs (Fonagy et al., 2002), just as they were not capable of mentalizing their own emotional experience. Hence, they were also incapable of sponsoring a space of "thirdness" (Benjamin, 2004, 2018) wherein both the child's and the parent's subjective experience can be held in mind by the parent (and ultimately the child) at the same time. The kinds of "collaborative dialogue" (back and forth attunements, adjustments, and repairs) one sees in videos of mothers and babies on their way to becoming securely attached (Lyons-Ruth, 1999; Beebe & Lachmann, 2014) were not possible in these patients' families. And such dialogical incompetence seems to have been the rule throughout later development, even with the introduction of language and expanding cognitive capacities. (See also Chapter 6 in this volume.)

This absence of intersubjective dialogue based on mutual recognition in the histories of coupled partners sets the stage for similar conditions in their adult relationship. For example, after chronic exposure to a partner's pejorative mis-mentalization of one's qualities or functioning in different domains, there is a tendency to unconsciously identify, at least to some degree, with that characterization. In the couple to be described in this chapter, the wife's experience growing up in a chaotic family predisposed her to diminishing the husband as a too harsh and not-to-be-trusted parent. Over many years, the husband, mostly unconsciously, came to identify with this attribution, even while consciously protesting it. He was susceptible to this kind of "internalization of negation," as he had been treated similarly by his dismissive, unloving mother. Such trauma histories set the stage for dialogical difficulties in adult coupled relationships where the unmet dependency and selfobject needs of childhood are unconsciously re-engaged; and analogues of the traumatic early frustration of those needs are re-experienced in the partners' transferences to each other.

In my experience, clinical and otherwise, I find that people tend to be unconsciously attracted to partners whose early histories and issues are similar to theirs in certain respects, even if their character organizations take ostensibly very different forms. A person who grew up in an airless world will tend to be drawn to a partner who has also experienced some form or degree of airlessness. At some unconscious level, they recognize each other. The co-created intersubjective systems that evolve in such partnered relationships are inescapably fraught with difficulties in the areas of recognition, self-recognition, empathy, self-expression, assertion, agency, and autonomy within a relational context; all of which tend to disable competent, constructive dialogue (especially in the crunch), and the capacity to restore dialogue when it breaks down.

The generalizations in the last paragraph do not always hold true. Some individuals with airless world histories do not recreate airless worlds in their relationships. (Psychoanalysis has always been better at postdiction than prediction!) An individual patient of mine with one of the most destructive and debilitating airless world histories I have encountered also has one of the strongest marriages. One reason for this is that her spouse grew up in a basically loving family and does not suffer from the same kind of negating internal objects that she does. Given her loving marriage in which she feels recognized and supported, she is readily able to engage in true dialogue and problem-solving with her partner, even as her profound self-negation continues to haunt and disable her in other contexts.

Nevertheless, in couples where both partners' individual historical airless worlds inform and underpin their uniquely co-created intersubjective world with each other, the above generalizations can help orient us to the kind of needed relationship we will seek to establish with such couples in therapy. We must somehow *meet* each of the partners in their individual experiences of airlessness, historically and in relation to each other, while, often simultaneously, seeking to introduce "air" into their dialogue *with* each other. One form this can take is through the idea of empathy: We try to empathize with each partner individually at the same time that we are trying to help them be more empathic with each other (Leone, 2021). The airless world model enables us, as therapists, to be empathic to each of the partners individually because of the dynamic/developmental understanding it offers; this, in turn, helps us help them become more understanding of, and empathic with, each other.

But in the way I think about empathy with couples, I believe there is also such a thing as *empathy with the relational system*: a progressive sense of where the couple system is working and where it is breaking down and, therefore, a kind of empathy with what the system "needs" at a given point in order to restore dialogue and connection—and really, viability. Often what is empathic to what the system needs at a given point is not synonymous with being empathic to the felt experience or needs of the individual partners, at least in the immediate present moment. I will illustrate what I mean here by looking at how I handled the first crisis that came up with the couple (introduced above) who presented after the husband's affair had come to light.

Jack and Ann: The Presenting Crisis

The couple, both successful professionals (Ann a psychiatrist and Jack a corporate attorney) in their early 50s, came to me referred by one of their individual therapists after a failed first attempt at couples therapy. That therapy broke down because Jack felt judged by the therapist for the affair. He admitted in our first session that it was hard for him to be open and honest with me, given the earlier experience. Ann agreed that the therapist hadn't focused enough on "how we got there." Though I thought I was mostly just listening non-judgmentally and taking notes, I must have shown enough genuine interest in their back story to have passed the first test. They arrived at the second session feeling, as Jack put it, "slightly hopeful about talking about key issues." Ann felt readier to do this too—she was somehow feeling less angry. She just wanted reassurance. At this point it became clear that Jack had not broken off the relationship with his affair partner, Eden. Ann wanted reassurance that Jack was ending things with Eden and was committed to staying and working on their relationship. He could not give her that reassurance—he still felt too ambivalent and distrusting of Ann's commitment to treating him differently. It was a revelation to Jack that he could be "something other than passive with her"—that he could "initiate dialogue about my feelings about her and how she has been treating me." Though I had not yet coined the term "airless world," I heard this as a statement that, even in their second session, Jack felt emboldened to express his true feelings in a more direct way for the first time—an indication that new "air" was already entering the system.

As is so often the case, the couple's core issues can be seen in retrospect to have been present in the first few sessions. For Ann, it was her profound hurt and abandonment issues, embodied in the insecurity she now felt about whether Jack still loved her or was going to leave her. For Jack, it was the root issues that had led to the affair: the fact that the two had "drifted apart" and been living "parallel lives," the way Ann had come to prioritize her relationships with their children over her relationship with him, and had, in his view, come to vilify him as the too harsh, unreliable parent. In short, Ann's core concern was her anxiety about being left, while Jack's was loneliness, hurt, and anger at the unloving, and ultimately intolerable, way he felt Ann had been treating him for years.

In the third session, Ann gave Jack an ultimatum about ending his relationship with Eden. He replied that he was thinking it over. She gave him one more week. He said he was "scared to put all my eggs in one basket—scared I'll get hurt." Jack said he realized he needed to give up Eden if he wanted to find out what was possible with Ann—he wanted to do that but didn't feel ready. The next session was extremely tense. Ann wanted him to make a firm commitment regarding Eden. He was only willing to say he was trying and was committed to working on this with Ann. She expressed how injured she felt by him: she was unsure if they were going to be able to figure it out. *I emphasized that they were talking about their conflict in a direct, honest way and that their ability to dialogue was most important in the long run.* Undoubtedly, that felt more reassuring to Jack than to Ann. I was aware of not yet feeling connected to either of them individually, but I did feel connected to them as a system, and very engaged in trying to hold and direct their system in ways that would help them navigate through their crisis.

The next few sessions were calmer, allowing me to stop the action long enough to get brief histories. I learned that Ann had grown up with a mentally ill mother in a chaotic family in which she had had to be precociously responsible. Jack, more like the patients I described in Chapter 1, had grown up feeling marginalized by a critical, controlling mother of five boys, "none of whom were important to her," and a weak father who could "neither stand up to my mother nor escape." These backgrounds—both airless worlds in different ways—helped explain their co-created, intersubjective airless world. Ann's over-protectiveness of her own children and need to make them her number-one priority made sense in light of the erratic, irresponsible, chaotic atmosphere she had had to survive with her mother. At the same time, her tendency to protect her kids from what she perceived to be Jack's unreliable and sometimes harsh treatment felt to Jack like cruel, unfair, marginalizing attacks, to which he could not effectively stand up, just as he had not been able to do with his controlling mother. Instead, he ultimately escaped. The affair seemed his only solution to the complete dialogue breakdown—read: airless world—they had been living in for years.

They remained in self-protective mode for several sessions, both being more reactive than proactive with each other, with no progress on their impasse. In the next session I weighed in more assertively, *confronting Jack with his need to make a clean break with Eden if he really wanted to see what was possible with Ann. I argued that if he wants Ann to make him a priority, he'll have to do the same with her.* I knew, and acknowledged, that this would not be a simple matter because Jack and Eden worked together on the same team in their law firm. Though Jack complained that he experienced me as siding with Ann here, there seemed to be progress by the next session. At the surface level Ann was still issuing her ultimatum, which still was making Jack feel like she was trying to control him. *I said I sensed some movement—I thought they were getting closer to being on the same page.* But Ann was so anxious about Jack's trustworthiness with Eden that she couldn't see any movement. At this point I made what, in retrospect, was the most critical intervention of their crisis: *I said I thought that whatever agreement they came to had to be bi-lateral, even though that seemed impossible.*

One only learns whether an intervention like this was helpful by tracking what happens over the next few sessions. In the next session Jack showed greater vulnerability: He said he needed to know if Ann still loved him. It was the feeling that she didn't that had pushed him toward the affair. He also said again that he experienced Ann's ultimatum as controlling. *I said I saw it less as controlling than as setting a limit on what she could tolerate. I also said his fear of being controlled was understandable, given his history with his mother.*

I then engaged Jack about how he could interact with Eden in a way that would set clear limits. *I said I thought he would need to be clear within himself about where to draw the line and how to avoid the slippery slope.* He got this, understood its importance, and conveyed that he was approaching being ready to do it. Following this conversation, between sessions, he and Ann moved closer in their language to an agreement, but Jack couldn't yet take out the word "try," much to Ann's dismay. *Here, I looked directly at Ann and said, in what I hoped she could hear as a caring voice, that for Jack to agree to any language as a compliance rather than something that was an expression of his own agency would not work.* By the following session, they came in having worked through to an agreement of intentions that was acceptable to both and allowed them to move forward. Jack immediately wanted to start addressing what he perceived as Ann's controlling-ness regarding his parenting over many years, at which point we were off to the races: We could begin to look more closely at the airless world they had been living in with each other prior to the affair.

Reflections on the Initial Crisis

When I saw this couple, I knew about airless world phenomena though I hadn't yet called them that (Stern, 2002a, 2002b). Just as they had been co-creating an airless world in their marriage for years—one that contained elements of the airless worlds both had grown up in—they were at high risk for repeating the same in the way they dealt with the crisis of the affair. The challenge was how to work with them around the crisis in such a way that they could be guided to do something different—to do something that not only helped them resolve their crisis but also gave them an experience of a less airless way of thinking and relating.

The starting point of our needed relationship was that I needed to quickly connect with Jack in such a way that he felt I was not going to hurt or humiliate him again and, in fact, might be able to help him. I did this mainly by taking seriously, and being curious about, the terrible feelings (of being unloved, marginalized, and unfairly vilified) which he believed led to his affair. I was not interested in judging—only in understanding what had happened. I didn't say this but apparently Jack felt it. At the same time, I knew Ann needed to feel that I got what she was going through and understood the urgency of what she needed Jack to do to reassure her. But I sensed she also realized that my first task (and significant challenge) was to connect with Jack and reassure him that this would be a safe space for him. I sensed that, even under these traumatizing conditions, she was willing to give me some leeway to achieve that. Jack arrived in therapy angry, distrustful, even paranoid, which caused me to be careful with him and, in general, careful about what I said and how I said things. I needed to establish a beginning alliance with him for our system to become viable. At the same time, I also sensed that both of them were there because they wanted their relationship to be repaired if possible. There was clearly still love on both sides, though that love had been seriously damaged. So, they were both motivated to have things work with me.

All of this organized itself around the crisis posed by Jack's continuing relationship with Eden and Ann's need for that relationship to end. At some level, everyone in the room knew that Jack had to end that relationship for Jack and Ann to begin to recover and engage with their underlying problems. But Jack had turned to Eden because of the felt airlessness in what his relationship with Ann had become. He felt that Ann had controlled things in their relationship and in their family, and that part of the way she had done that was to make him the bad one and thereby marginalize and weaken him. The affair had been his desperate attempt to find needed air, which had succeeded to some extent. And he was not about to return to that same lonely, humiliating airless world with Ann. He was angry and was not doing things on her terms anymore.

My main insight—really more of an intuition—was that even though ultimately Ann was right—Jack had to end the affair—any viable resolution of their impasse had to be a negotiation in which both of their subjectivities played a part and to which both could authentically agree. In other words, it had to be a "breathable" agreement. That stance might have seemed to privilege Jack's position and needs more than Ann's, and ran the risk of Ann feeling that I, another man, was taking the betrayal, the continuing "crime," and the intolerability of her position, too lightly. But truly, I did get that and wasn't siding with either: I was siding with the system—seeking to make it more "competent" (Russell, 2006; Sander, 2008) going forward. I might describe my strategy as trying to insert a *new principle* into their system—the principle that (1) both of their subjectivities, both of their personal agencies, had to be incorporated into their dialogue and problem-solving process; and that (2) it wouldn't kill either of them to be more direct or to be the recipient of the other's directness. And I had to introduce this new principle in such a way that both experienced me as taking *their* experience, needs, and sensitivities into account (well enough) and creating a space in which both could "breathe." Neither of them had ever lived in a space like that—a space where the authority figures insisted on intersubjective relating in Benjamin's (2004, 2018) sense of taking into account both one's own and the other's different subjectivities. I think my effort to begin to establish that kind of space caused them to come out of that first crisis and phase in our work trusting that we were co-creating a space where something different could happen in their marriage.

Navigating, Negotiating, Challenging, and Holding the Impossible

There is obviously not space to provide a detailed account of the four-year treatment that followed the resolution of Jack and Ann's initial crisis. By the time they felt ready to terminate, they had worked through their most problematic issues and arrived in a much better, more "breathable" space with each other. They had managed to air and process their major hurts and resentments to the point of making a true mutual commitment to their marriage going forward. And they were much better at having real intersubjective dialogue around their most fraught issues.

Even now, many years following their termination, I am surprised at the positive outcome. I remember that I often felt surprised when they would come in after a difficult session, or series of sessions, suddenly, and seemingly inexplicably, in a better place. I think this has to do with the nature of airless world problems in couples: There is a certain feeling or quality of *impossibility* and the consequent nature of the therapeutic task, which is to be able, paradoxically, to hold the sense of impossibility while at the same time challenging it. When I think of my work with Jack and Ann, it feels like I was engaged in a kind of "dance with their system" in which I tried, opportunistically and in different ways, to simultaneously hold them and push against their system so as to create new spaces for the introduction of psychic air. To do this sometimes meant saying things that felt threatening to one or both of them, and then being able to tolerate their upset or anger with me for what they experienced as my criticizing or attacking them. At such points, it could feel like our therapeutic system was also becoming airless—like the just impossible was becoming *really* impossible. But I can see, looking back, that my job was to be able to hold the "really impossible" as well as the "just impossible." I will share a few additional vignettes from their four-year treatment to give the flavor of what I'm trying to convey.

Because both had grown up in families where their true needs and feelings had been ruthlessly, or heedlessly, negated, and both had learned to accommodate to the powerful other as a requirement for psychic survival (Brandshaft, 2010), neither saw the direct expression of needs and feelings as a fathomable option. Being on the giving *or* receiving end of such directness could feel re-traumatizing to both Jack and Ann. Thus, when Ann expressed her angry feelings about Jack's affair, she became immediately terrified that her complaints would drive him back to Eden. "*Maybe,*" I said at one point, "*but it seems unlikely, given Jack's commitment to making things work between you.*" Similarly, when Jack expressed his resentment at how Ann had portrayed him as a parent, Ann could easily fragment at such criticism. On one occasion *I told her that I thought she was over-generalizing Jack's criticism and that I thought he needed to be able to express these feelings*. Though she said nothing in response, my sense was that it made a small difference going forward.

When Ann was able to start directly expressing her loving feelings toward Jack, he felt mostly wary and paranoid, thinking she was trying to manipulate him into voicing the same feelings in return. When Jack was able to start expressing his loving feelings toward Ann, he did it in such a hesitant and understated way that it left Ann still insecure and in need of more explicit reassurance, which Jack felt unable and unwilling to give. At the end of one such session, *I confronted Jack with what I thought was his need to reassure Ann about his commitment even if he didn't yet totally feel it the way she needed to hear it.* He didn't like this and said he didn't want this to start feeling like their earlier therapy (in which the therapist had sided with Ann and shamed Jack for his infidelity). Yet, surprisingly, Jack arrived at their next session wanting to "talk about what we like and love about each other!" He spontaneously started saying that he likes her because of her familiarity; he likes being with her. To which she immediately responded by saying she feels he's important—she cares about him, wouldn't choose to live without him. She then said she wanted to hear him say the same. Unexpectedly, rather than protesting, he admitted that he needed to hear Ann say *she* loves *him*—he had felt pushed away for so many years. This, to me, was a surprising and moving turn after eight months of mostly standoffs on these questions. I didn't love my confrontation of Jack—encouraging him to say something he might not consciously feel yet. And he didn't like it either. But somehow, he, and they, were able to use it to take the next risk. Somehow the confrontation had introduced a little psychic air.

By the following session, Jack was back complaining about Ann's excessive need for reassurance, still experiencing this as controlling. They quickly resumed their defensive standoff, and again *I started to feel like I couldn't see my way through their impasse. I noted but didn't say out loud that both need to realize this will not come easily. There's much pain on the way to re-connection. The good news is, you're both committed!* This whole sequence—both the spoken and the unspoken—is an example of what I mean by "dancing with the system."

By our third year they were in a significantly better place, which meant that their pattern of oscillation between anxious/angry standoff and tentative expression of positive feelings no longer had the airless, existentially dire ("impossible") quality. Everyone had relaxed a bit, but this didn't mean that all was well. Jack was doing some critical work in his individual therapy around coming to terms with the airlessness in his family growing up. He was in an intense grief process in relation to both parents, especially his mother. He felt very angry and "needed space" to process it all. Ann, the eternal helper, wanted him to talk to her about it. But this irritated Jack. He didn't want to be told by Ann how to process his own grief. This gets into the area of *negotiation*, which I included in the title of this section. There was a constant, always difficult process of negotiation going on between what each of them felt they needed from the other and what the other could tolerate (see also Pizer, 1998). *I felt part of my job was to feel my way into the negotiation impasses and try to open up the closed spaces.*

In a session during this period, Ann was expressing her insecurity and need for Jack to show more love, more interest in sex. Jack remained in his self-focused, self-protective mode, angry still about the years of "begging for sex." He did acknowledge, though, that he felt they were in a better place now. I took this as a cue that Jack might be ready to be gently challenged. *I said I thought he needed to attend to the relationship—what they needed as a couple—as well as to his own self-protection. I added that if he didn't, Ann would come after him for reassurance. I also told Ann I thought her wish for reassurance and commitment was understandable but expressing it might not be in touch with where Jack was now. I also told her for the first time that I didn't think reassurance could come only from the outside—from Jack. Ultimately, she would need to be able to calm and reassure herself.* This kind of balancing, or weaving (Shaddock, 2023), intervention is not unique to airless couples. But I found myself doing a lot of it with Jack and Ann, constantly nudging them to renegotiate what was possible between them, and what was possible for them to tolerate hearing from me.

My message to Ann here reflected a general principle which I felt was essential to their ever getting to a place of more comfortable intersubjective relating. That would require a greater *separation* between them, such that they were not so desperately looking to the other for primary validation and empowerment. Their constant orientations to the perceived messages coming from the other were holdovers from their traumatic childhoods in which basic needs for empathic attunement and affirmation of selfhood had never been met, or worse, had been systematically negated. Thus, part of their archaic transferences to each other included both the conscious and unconscious transfer of these early needs, and the power these transferences gave the other as the controller of their fate and experience of self. *As our therapy progressed, I embedded more explicit messages about their need to be able to separate from this dependent bond with each other and become their "own person" as a condition for a healthier connection.* This was not a holdover from the bad old days of one-person psychology and the myth of the autonomous self. It came from my understanding of the impediments to healthy separation-individuation in individuals who had grown up in airless world conditions (see Chapter 1). Fortunately, they were both in individual therapies that could provide in-depth work in this area that was synergistic with what we were doing in couples therapy.

The final sequence I will share began with my directly, though gently, confronting Jack regarding his tendency often to lead with a sarcastic edge. Jack's sarcasm, a form of turning passive into active, was a street tactic he had developed as a defense in the couple's decades-long war with each other prior to therapy; though it probably also reflected a cynical, passive-aggressive, somewhat paranoid response to the war-like conditions of his childhood. Since things were in fact getting better between Ann and him, his sarcasm was feeling like a vestigial lag, which I thought was functioning like one of Gottman's (1994) "four horsemen of the apocalypse" in terms of its destructive effects on their connection. *I said, as tactfully as I could, that his sarcasm conveyed a "baseline irritability and hostility" that was not helping their efforts to improve their dialogue.* Ann was quick to agree that his sarcasm always felt critical and that she was highly reactive to it. Jack did not like this at all and left the session angry. In the next session, he came back and said he felt attacked by me last week and considered not returning to therapy. "Like, why am I doing this?!" But then a subtle shift took place wherein he was expressing his anger at me directly. *He said he felt I had accused him of being angry when he wasn't. I said I hadn't meant to imply that—I was trying to address his sarcastic style in general. But then I realized, and said, that this was an example of how his sarcastic tone was now getting in the way: He in fact had not been angry, but his sarcastic tone made it sound like he was.* In the end, amazingly, there was a sense of re-connection and mutual appreciation between Jack and me following this openly confrontational conversation. By the next week, he still felt "raw and wary" after our encounter, but he talked about it again. His takeaway was that he needed to assume more responsibility for not standing up for himself and getting into a "one-up/one-down," "winner-loser" position with people. One week later, they reported doing much better. Ann was working on her "anxiety," trying not to grill him. Jack was trying not to "snipe" at her. The tone between them was far more "loving and gentle." Air was creeping in!

Conclusion

This is not mainly a chapter about clinical technique. The way I worked with Jack and Ann felt highly specific to their relationship and our therapeutic system. It was, however, informed by my understanding of airless world phenomena. Not only were both Jack and Ann unable psychically to breathe, they didn't know how to breathe. They had never lived in a psychically, intersubjectively breathable space, so neither could imagine how they needed to be different with each other (and with themselves) in order to engage in mutually sustainable dialogue. The initial problem was how to meet them where they were but, pretty quickly, bring them into sufficiently intersubjective dialogue so that they could work through and resolve their presenting crisis. I was going mainly by feel: If I was the needed psychic ventilator and relational life-support, how and where could I introduce "air" into their airless system?

The answer lay not only in what I did per se, but in how I was *holding* what I was doing. Though I felt I needed to exert a certain "force" to interrupt their long-standing doer/done-to patterns, it was crucial that I did so without judgment and without *needing* them to change. Though I had to be clear that change was necessary, they couldn't feel that I was narcissistically invested in their changing. I also sensed I had to lead by example—by being firm about certain things, and assertive in certain ways, but always with an empathic intention to meet them where they were and in ways I hoped they could hear and use. I had to be comfortable operating from my own sense of therapeutic agency, which meant being prepared for their reactions. Thus, I was firm about the necessity of both partners having to authentically agree to the terms of their resolution of Jack's continued involvement with Eden. But I was also assertive with Jack that, if he wanted things to work with Ann, he would have to give up Eden. Ann didn't love the first intervention; Jack didn't love the second. I didn't need them to love what I was saying—in fact, I viewed any complaints as a form of psychic breathing on their part in relation to me. But I hoped that the way I was doing it, including my comfort with their objections, would begin to model a different way of being and interacting in tense, conflictual situations—a way of interacting in which both parties are able to speak and breathe.

This basic approach became more complex and nuanced as the therapy progressed past the initial crisis into the four-year project and process of introducing psychic air into their chronically airless marital world. I described this process as "navigating, negotiating, challenging, and holding the impossible." I hope the foregoing vignettes give a sense of what I'm trying to convey with this characterization. Though things did indeed feel impossible at times, it was important that I be able to hold the feeling of impossibility "without memory or desire" (Bion, 1970)—that is, with a kind of paradoxical acceptance that things really do seem impossible now coupled with a vague faith that if we stay with it, something different might become possible.

In hindsight, I believe that the crux of therapeutic action in this case was a "system trust" that Jack and Ann developed with me over time. They didn't totally trust me to be empathic and protective with each of them individually at all times; but they were increasingly trusting of my intention and ability to take care of them as a couple—as a system. Because of that developing system trust, they became increasingly willing and able to make use of my efforts to help them.

References

Alvarez, A. (2012). *The thinking heart: Three levels of psychoanalytic therapy with disturbed children*. London: Routledge.

Beebe, B., & Lachmann, F.M. (2014). *The origins of attachment: Infant research and adult treatment*. London: Routledge.

Benjamin, J. (2004). Beyond doer and done to: An intersubjective view of thirdness. *Psychoanalytic Quarterly, 73*: 5–46.

Benjamin, J. (2018). *Beyond doer and done to: Recognition theory, intersubjectivity and the third*. London and New York, NY: Routledge.

Bion, W.R. (1970). *Attention and interpretation*. London: Karnac.

Brandchaft, B. (2010). Toward an emancipatory psychoanalysis. In B. Brandchaft, S. Doctors, & D. Sorter (Eds.), *Toward an emancipatory psychoanalysis: Brandchaft's intersubjective vision* (pp. 9–27). New York, NY and London: Routledge.

Cooney, A.S. (2018). Vitalizing enactment: A relational exploration. *Psychoanalytic Dialogues, 28*: 340–354.

Ferenczi, S. (1933). Confusion of tongues between adults and the child. In M. Balint (Ed.), *Final contributions to the problems and methods of psychoanalysis* (pp. 156–167). London: Karnac.

Fonagy, P., Gergely, G., Jurist, E.L., & Target, M. (2002). *Affect regulation, mentalization, and the development of the self*. New York, NY: Other Press.

Gottman, J. (1994). *Why marriages succeed or fail...and how you can make yours last.* New York, NY: Simon & Schuster Paperbacks.

Green, A. (1983/1997). The dead mother. In A. Green (Ed.), *On private madness* (pp. 142—173). London: Karnac Books.

Harris, A. (2019). Discussion: "Airless worlds: The traumatic sequelae of identification with parental negation" by Steven Stern. *Psychoanalytic Dialogues, 29*: 451–459.

Leone, C. (2021). The application of contemporary self-psychology to couple therapy. *Couple and Family Psychoanalysis, 11*(2): 170–186.

Lyons-Ruth, K. (1999). The two-person unconscious: Intersubjective dialogue, enactive relational representation, and the emergence of new forms of relational organization. *Psychoanalytic Inquiry, 19*: 576–617.

Mahler, M., Pine, F., & Bergman, A. (1975). *The psychological birth of the human infant: Symbiosis and individuation.* New York, NY: Basic Books.

Pizer, S.A. (1998). *Building bridges: The negotiation of paradox in psychoanalysis.* Hillsdale, NJ: The Analytic Press.

Russell, P.L. (2006). The theory of the crunch. In P.L. Russell (Ed.), *Smith college studies in social work, Volume 26* (pp. 9–21). New York, NY: Haworth Press.

Sander, L. (2002). Thinking differently: Principles of process in living systems and the specificity of being known. *Psychoanalytic Dialogues, 12*: 11–42.

Shaddock, D. (2023). A triadic developmental system: Implications of infant research for couples therapy. (English version) *Psychoanalysis, Self and Context, 3*: 190–200.

Stern, S. (2002a). The self as a relational structure: A dialogue with multiple-self theory. *Psychoanalytic Dialogues, 12*: 693–714.

Stern, S. (2002b). Identification, repetition, and psychological growth: An expansion of relational theory. *Psychoanalytic Psychology, 19*: 722–738.

Stern, S. (2013). *Psychodynamic couples therapy.* Paper presented at Psychiatry Grand Rounds, Maine Medical Center, December 3, 2013.

Stern, S. (2019). Airless worlds: The traumatic sequelae of identification with parental negation. *Psychoanalytic Dialogues, 29*: 435–450.

Wallin, D. (2007). *Attachment and psychotherapy.* New York, NY: Guilford.

Weiss, J., Sampson, H., & The Mount Zion Psychotherapy Research Group. (1986). *The psychoanalytic process: Theory, clinical observations and empirical research.* New York, NY: Guildford Press.

Chapter 5

Analytic Adoption of the Psychically Homeless

Nearly every victim of a severe neurosis displays eventually the disposition to be "adopted."…An ideal arrangement would be something like a huge home for "homeless children"; probably such an idea is quite fantastic, but at least its equivalent must be provided in a psychic sense, by a feeling on the part of the analyst that provides in the immaterial but powerful realm of the mind succor and support for a "homeless" psyche. "Wandering souls" they are, all suffering internally from a lack of the sense of security, and very often from a lack of the sense of reality as well—people whose personalities have been "split," or at least injured, by some events and conditions beyond their control and usually forgotten.

Elizabeth Severn, *The Discovery of the Self* (1933/2017)[1]

Some of our patients arrive in our practices in states of psychic homelessness. Their childhood memories tell stories of unfathomable neglect, abuse, parental hatred, and psychotic renderings of this child as a bad object, unwanted, undeserving of love and attention, defective, or contemptibly difficult and needy. At a lesser extreme, the parents may not have been manifestly destructive but were so narcissistically self-focused, even as they may have tried to provide their idea of good parenting, that the child remained emotionally alone with no parental "ears" or "eyes" capable of hearing or seeing their true psychic realities or needs. Of course, our patients' histories are complex and unique, often with good elements in the mix. My point is that for some, their early family environments were so far from "good enough" that they were, and remain, emotional orphans left with profound conscious and unconscious longings for a new relational home wherein they would feel, for the first time, a sense of belonging.

DOI: 10.4324/9781003585237-6

Consider my patient Elizabeth, a woman I saw for 40 years. During the first ten years of our work, which included five hospitalizations, I gradually learned that she had been massively abused—sexually, physically, and emotionally—by her sociopathic, alcoholic father, and viewed as a messenger from the devil by her nearly psychotic mother—a mother who never wanted her and in fact was happy the night her water broke, thinking it meant she was having a miscarriage. Elizabeth remembered, as a child, wandering around her neighborhood at dusk, looking into the windows of the homes of other families as they were eating dinner and wishing she belonged to one of those normal-seeming families. The new-object-seeking impulse contained in this wishful fantasy was the same one that animated the profound new-object transference she was able to establish with me virtually from the beginning of our analytic work.

I have found that with certain of my patients, Elizabeth being a prime example, long-term analytic treatment offers the possibility of what I term "mutual analytic adoption,"[2] and with it a deep sense of belonging. The concept first occurred to me when I was writing a discussion of Joye Weisel-Barth's 2011 paper, "Katherine: A Long, Hard Case," for the *International Journal of Psychoanalytic Self Psychology* (Weisel-Barth, 2011; Stern, 2011). The author and her patient shared a 30-year-plus treatment, one that had been at times stormy, but in the end was transformative. In that treatment, Weisel-Barth had done a number of things that lay outside our traditional notions of the analytic frame. On one occasion she took the patient, who was in a suicidal state, to the hospital herself, then took care of the patient's young daughter for the rest of the afternoon. Years later she bought this same daughter, now an adolescent and a gifted musician, an instrument because her patient had become disabled by an accident and fallen on hard times. I thought these "interventions," though controversial and risky, remained analytic because they did not violate the essential asymmetry of the analytic relationship (Aron, 1991; Hoffman, 1998). But more than this, they reflected Weisel-Barth's personal investment in Katherine and contributed to what amounted to a mutual analytic adoption that was life-saving for her. Katherine, an immigrant with a childhood as horrific as my patient Elizabeth's, actually came to think of Weisel-Barth as her "American mother."

I wrote the first version of this chapter as a paper for a 2014 conference in Jerusalem sponsored by the International Association of Psychoanalytic

Self Psychology, the theme of which was: "Belonging: Where Do We Call Home?" This theme prompted me to give my nascent ideas about analytic adoption further thought. Thinking about my practice over the years, I realized there were degrees of analytic adoption, reflecting the unique needs of the patient and the unique qualities and trajectory of my relationship with each patient with whom I felt some sense of analytic adoption had taken place. Accordingly, I saw a need for more of a theory, or at least a delineation of the principles involved, in order to understand and explain the workings of these processes across a range of cases. This chapter represents my attempt to articulate these principles.

Because my relationship with Elizabeth, which was still ongoing at the time of the Jerusalem conference, included frequent meta-communication about our therapeutic relationship, I told her about this project and asked her to share any thoughts she had about the idea of belonging. She came in with a list of salient elements she thought had contributed to her feeling of belonging in our relationship. I will, for the moment, just list her thoughts and words because they are so germane and evocative.

She started with: "Belonging is *your coming here*." This referred to the fact that I had moved to Maine from Chicago 11 years earlier and continued to travel to Chicago one weekend a month to see my remaining patients there. It was clear to both of us that these visits signified my caring and commitment above what might be typical in this situation. (More later on the impact of my move on our "adoptive" relationship.) To continue with her list, she wrote: "*safety, love, investment, shelter, assurance, acceptance of need, exhilarating and frightening, relaxed vs. anxious, rooted, essential to life and growth, mutual, respectful, clean air, commitment, security, trust, real, unique*." She also said that in the long period that preceded the sense of security that comes with analytic adoption she had felt like she was in analytic "foster care." That is, she was always worried that she might say or do something, or need too much, such that I would want to get rid of her. Her final thought was that it is the sense of belonging that makes it possible, ultimately, to *let go*.

The Need for a Relational Home

I am not the first to suggest that patients who have been relationally traumatized as children come to treatment needing what Robert Stolorow (2006) felicitously called a "relational home." This notion echoes the

thinking of a number of earlier relationally oriented psychoanalytic pio-
neers, especially Ferenczi, Winnicott, and Loewald. Stolorow defined what
he meant by a relational home in a particular way. He argued that patients
who have grown up with parents who were "grossly mal-attuned" to their
emotional experience and therefore unable to give verbal expression to
this experience require a therapeutic relationship that performs just this
"somatic-symbolic integrative function." He wrote that it is only through a
therapeutic process in which "emotional experience comes into language…
that the sense of being is born." Stolorow (2014) has subsequently added a
further dimension of the relational home required by severely traumatized
patients: what he calls "emotional dwelling." In emotional dwelling, the
analyst not only welcomes the patient's dissociated affects and pre-reflec-
tive organizing assumptions, they accompany the patient in an undiluted
encounter with (a not-turning-away-from) the overwhelmingly painful
affects and memories of trauma and loss. While I agree with Stolorow that
these functions are critical for this group of patients, and certainly played
a major role in my treatment of Elizabeth, I don't think they fully capture
all of the elements our psychically homeless patients may require in order
to experience analytic treatment as a relational home or to experience the
sense of belonging for which they are desperately searching. Delineating
what constitutes a relational home in this deeper, more personal sense
requires a relational theory that captures the elements my patient Elizabeth
jotted down on a piece of paper after 36 years in treatment.

Among the major theorists who have written in this area, Winnicott
came closest to theorizing and actually offering his patients many of the elements I have in mind. In a paper entitled "How D.W. Winnicott Conducted
Psychoanalysis," James Anderson (2014) characterized Winnicott's
approach based on his own reading of Winnicott and, importantly, the
actual experiences of some of Winnicott's famous patients as described in
their writings and/or in personal interviews conducted by Anderson. These
first-hand accounts reveal the quality or spirit of work I'm trying to capture
in this paper.

Margaret Little (1985) wrote "Literally, through many long hours he
held my two hands clasped between his, almost like an umbilical cord,
while I lay, often hidden beneath the blanket, silent, inert, withdrawn, in
panic, rage or tears, asleep and sometimes dreaming" (cited in Anderson,
2014, p. 383). Rosemary Dinnage recalled that "I was crying one time and
he put his hands out and said, 'Cry on my hands'" (p. 384). Based on his

interview with her, Anderson noted that Dinnage was uncomfortable with physical contact, and Winnicott's gesture and words empathically took that into account. Both Dinnage and Little spoke about Winnicott's adjusting the length of the sessions to their needs: usually an hour and a half, but sometimes longer. "There was no doctrine," Little said, "no ritual beyond what an individual patient needed (e.g., handshaking, helping on with coat, cup of coffee at session end)...Humanness was all-important" (p. 386). Guntrip (1975) recalled that Winnicott had told him: "I'm good for you but you're good for me...You don't have to be good for me. I don't need it and can cope without it, but in fact you are good for me." Guntrip took from this that Winnicott was like a new "mother who could value her child, so that I could cope with what was to come" (p. 389).

Winnicott had a unique style and patterned his particular kind of relational home after his ideas about the mother–infant relationship. What I want to emphasize in these quotes is not so much the specific interventions but the way Winnicott *blended the clinical and the personal* in his therapeutic approach, and how crucial this was to his patients' experience of being reached and helped. I hear, in the subtext of their narratives, a feeling of deep, authentic belonging—a sense of having found a relational home they had never experienced—which Winnicott engendered through the highly personalized therapeutic relationship he offered each of them. Note that I am emphasizing equally the clinical *and* the personal. Winnicott's patients not only felt welcomed and personally responded to, they felt deeply understood. Indeed, these two components are inextricable: The relational home Winnicott established with each patient grew out of his understanding of them as well as the more implicit forms of being and relating that evolved between them.

Three General Principles

Generalizing from Winnicott's example, I suggest that in treating psychically homeless patients there are three major principles. By "principles" I don't mean an intentional method or something the analyst *tries* to do, exactly. It is more at the level of analytic sensibility and the analyst's presence in the relationship.

The first key principle is that it is not enough for the therapist to be, or think of themselves as being, a *responder* to the patient's therapeutic needs. Even frame-stretching concepts like Winnicott's (1965) "adaptation to need,"

Orange's (1995) "emotional availability," Corpt's (2011) "clinical generosity," and Pizer's (2008, 2014) "generous involvement" don't fully capture what I believe our psychologically homeless patients need from us (and what Winnicott actually offered his patients). They need us to be empathic, emotionally generous responders, to be sure, but more than that they also need us to be *active agents* who come to feel a personal investment in them. In other words, such a patient needs to feel actively *wanted* and, in a sense, *claimed* by the therapist, not just that the therapist is performing their job of responding empathically to the patient's needs and/or demands, or even skillfully grasping and illuminating the patient's subjective and intersubjective worlds.

This is a complex principle because of the fine line between wanting or claiming the patient *in an analytic way* and having a need or agenda to induct the patient into a preconceived role relationship, including, in the extreme, a blurring or transgression of the analytic relationship and frame. *Claiming* in an analytic sense grows out of the recognition that the patient had very little good parenting and thus is in need of a kind of re-parenting—the unique kind that analysis can provide and that Winnicott was the first (since Ferenczi's early experiments) to articulate explicitly. As part of this recognition, the analyst understands that in certain crucial ways the analyst, as Orange (2012) has written, may have to "go first" in taking the risks involved in deepening the analytic engagement. In an analytic context, this initiative or risk-taking must emerge as a natural part of a two-person, often highly complex, dance that is really a *mutual* claiming. Moreover, this mutual claiming develops in a context that frequently involves repetition, re-traumatization, and resistance on both sides to the mutual adoption process. In this sense, analytic adoption should not be overly romanticized. It can be, as it was in Weisel-Barth's work with Katherine, very messy, turbulent, and marked by unpredictable impasses and setbacks.

This first principle of the analyst as an active agent who, over time, comes to claim the patient as part of a mutual claiming process is a variant of the larger topic of "analytic love," which has been written about by many, including myself in my original discussion of Weisel-Barth's paper on Katherine (Stern, 2011). (See also Frankel, 1993; Davies, 1994; Bach, 2006; Fosshage, 2007; Mendelsohn, 2007; Slavin, 2007; Hoffman, 2009; and Shaw, 2014, on the topic of analytic love.) While I believe analytic love, however one defines it, is an essential contributor to therapeutic action in any long-term analytic treatment, mutual analytic adoption takes analytic love to a different level and comes into play in cases where psychic homelessness has been a life-long reality for the patient. The principle of mutual claiming also has continuities with George Atwood's (2012) concept of "radical engagement," which grew out of his career-long project of understanding and treating psychotic patients.

The second principle, related to the first, is that in cases of mutual analytic adoption there is often a *blurring or loosening of the boundary between the professional role relationship and a more personal relationship of authentic mutual investment and caring*. This is also a complex principle, saturated with paradoxes. It is no accident that Winnicott, the theorist who placed the holding of such paradoxes at the center of his analytic sensibility, was so seemingly comfortable with the loosening of this boundary.

The main paradox is that the loosening or blurring I'm referring to does not violate the fundamental frame and asymmetry of the analytic relationship (Aron, 1991; Hoffman, 1998). The blurring or blending in fact depends on the essential safety that this frame and asymmetry assures. This basic frame does place limits on the personal mutual involvement of patient and analyst and poses conundrums that the analytic pair must struggle with. I will return to a consideration of these conundrums as they emerged at various points in my treatment of Elizabeth.

The third principle has to do with the *experience of time* in cases of mutual analytic adoption, and *how the relationship exists in time*. If we are to respond to a psychically homeless patient's need for a relational home, this holds implications for our *availability* to meet the patient in ways that do not always fit comfortably within even our more flexible ideas about the analytic frame and analytic time frames. Much in the spirit of Bass (2007), the frame will need to be a unique and evolving co-creation—one which holds the paradox of the two participants being part of each other's lives without *really* becoming part of each other's lives outside the therapy relationship. Not only might this paradox play out in the patient's need for the therapist's time between sessions, it affects how one thinks about the relationship as it exists over time. If there has been something like a mutual analytic adoption, the question may arise as to why the relationship should end before one party is no longer able to participate.

Theoretical Context

All three of these principles grow out of a more general clinical philosophy articulated in my 2017 book, *Needed Relationships and Psychoanalytic*

Healing. Central to this needed-relationship sensibility is the idea of *meeting the patient.* This idea, which has its roots in Winnicott's (1962, 1965) precept of making "a live adaptation to each patient's needs," has been elaborated within a contemporary nonlinear dynamic systems framework by the developmental researcher and theorist, Louis Sander (1995, 2008) in a series of now familiar principles he grouped together under the rubric of what he called *recognition process.* These include his concepts: *moments of meeting; specificity of recognition; specificity of connection;* and *the progressive achievement of relational fittedness* within an asymmetrical two-person system. (See also Bacal with Carlson, 2011, for further elaboration of the principle of specificity). Seen within this broader framework, the three principles I am proposing all grow out of the general idea of meeting the psychically homeless patient in such a way as to co-create the necessary conditions for the development of a secure sense of belonging and a meaningful psychological life.

Scenes from an Analytic Adoption: A 40-Year Odyssey

Elizabeth and I met in 1978 in Madison, Wisconsin, where I was a psychology intern and she a college sophomore and refugee from a profoundly dysfunctional family in small-town Wisconsin. Earnest and bright, and, remarkably, able to form a trusting attachment to me very quickly, there was a frightened, squirrel-like quality to her presence and emotional reactivity. Though she managed to get straight As, her personal life was chaotic, and her tenuous separation from her family (who lived only an hour away) kept her in the orbit of their destructive, unpredictable, crazy-making influence.

The memory from our long relationship that stood out for Elizabeth more than any other occurred in the winter of 1979, only a few months after we had started our twice-a-week therapy. She had just made a suicide attempt, and, after leaving her a note saying that I would be there, I visited her in the hospital. When I got up to leave and zipped up my down parka, I spontaneously hugged her—a real bear hug that lasted more than a second or two. This hug, aside from its intrinsic therapeutic effects, signified to Elizabeth that I had gone beyond my role-based behavior to let her know I was *really* there for her.

Possessed, somehow, of the determination to create a healthier life for herself than anything she had witnessed growing up, after a number of exploitive sexual relationships with much older men, Elizabeth fell in love with, and ultimately married, Tom, the brilliant son of an internationally prominent scientist. Tom had his own issues, given his ice-cold, controlling mother with a limitless superiority complex. A refugee in a different sense, Tom chose, in Elizabeth, someone who was emotionally available and kind, even though his mother looked down on her for being from the wrong side of the tracks. The two shared a sense of personal ethics and relational integrity that would be hard to explain, given both of their backgrounds. When Tom finished law school, he chose a clerkship in Chicago where I had moved a year earlier. This allowed Elizabeth to resume treatment with me after a one-year hiatus.

Elizabeth's most profound difficulties throughout our long relationship were in the areas of self- and affect-regulation. The abuse she had experienced at the hands of her father was enough to have permanently damaged her self-regulatory capacities. But the worst damage may have been wrought by her mother, who was the opposite of soothing: If, as a young child, Elizabeth had a normal need of any kind, the mother's visceral, automatic response was to feel acutely burdened and resentful. Elizabeth was the third of four children and, for some reason, the one the mother identified as the bad, unwanted, diabolical child. In a model scene that Elizabeth remembers from around age six, she was sitting on the stairs alone, crying and screaming. Her mother's reaction was to become enraged with *her*, dragging her into the bathroom and pushing her head under water in the toilet, causing Elizabeth to think she was going to die. One of the legacies of this early period was that she lived in a constant state of tension and fear, which could morph into panic in an instant. When these states became intolerable, Elizabeth learned that making herself throw up had a calming effect. So this became a primary mechanism of self-regulation.

Elizabeth's father ensured her compliance with his sexual violations through intimidation and fear, sometimes threatening her at knifepoint. He also used degradation and shaming—telling her he chose her instead of her younger sister because she looked like a dog. She remembers being mortified that somehow there would be evidence on her body of their shameful activities. Thus, another self-regulatory behavior was washing herself over and over in the shower with Lava soap, seeking to cleanse herself of her shameful, disgusting contamination.

I go into this uncomfortable level of detail to provide the context for my decision *to make myself available by phone between sessions as needed.* After Elizabeth moved to Chicago, we began meeting five times a week, but she needed much more. Here is where the reverberating question of *time* first came into play. The prevailing analytic wisdom in the mid-1980s was that patients needed to be able to work within the therapeutic structure—indeed, maintaining those limits, and interpreting patients' difficulties operating within them, were considered central to therapeutic action with patients like Elizabeth. Influenced by Kernberg's (1975) philosophy of treating borderlines, and fearful of fostering what Balint (1968) had termed "malignant regression," my inclination, initially, was to set limits—not so much on the calls themselves, but by ending them after what I deemed a reasonable length of time—usually 10–15 minutes. My hope was that such limit-setting would have the containing, ultimately calming effect the prevailing theory predicted it would. Instead, Elizabeth would come into the next session after such a call as frantic as I had left her the night before, and would likely call me later in the day in the same state.

Fearful that I was in fact fostering a malignant regression, I sought supervision with the best consultant I could find—Kenny Newman, a respected Chicago analyst whom I knew to be influenced by Kohut and Winnicott (See Newman et al., 1988). Newman listened for a couple of weeks, then made a radical suggestion. He said, "Why don't you try waiting till *she's* ready to end the call—I think it will work out better for both of you!" I thought, "That's easy for you to say!" But he turned out to be prescient. In the next call, I relinquished my preconception of how long I thought the call should reasonably take and waited to see what happened. After about half an hour Elizabeth felt settled enough that she was able to end the call. Surprisingly, she came to her session the next day not only still feeling calm, but also grateful to me for staying with her on the phone until she felt understood and settled. And, equally surprisingly, it was at least a week until something (either in session or out) had disrupted her again, requiring her to call me needing a similar kind of empathic, patient, regulatory interchange which took as long as it took.

What had Newman understood that mainstream psychoanalytic wisdom was missing? The radical idea that flew in the face of prevailing analytic theory was that the patient could actually be *trusted* to know what she needed (implicitly if not exactly consciously) and trusted not to simply use the analyst's availability to act out regressive drive wishes or malignant needs. Kohut (1971, 1977) had written about recognizing and accepting the patient's selfobject needs and longings, but hadn't covered situations like mine with Elizabeth that went beyond what the analyst could provide empathically during the session. Across the ocean, Winnicott (1965) had written about adapting technique to the patient's legitimate needs, which, as noted earlier, included lengthening session times, physical holding, and personal disclosures such as his comment to Guntrip: "I'm good for you, but you're also good for me." Drawing on this new "hermeneutic of trust," as Orange (2011) would term it many years later, Newman saw that Elizabeth lacked the capacity to calm herself during panic states or angry tantrums. He understood that the selfobject bond she had formed with me and my availability to stay with her emotionally when that bond was still insufficiently internalized to hold her in her more fragmented states were the necessary means for her psychoanalytic growth. The rub was that this meant giving Elizabeth a lot of time—indeed, it required a radical alteration in how I thought about the nature of psychoanalytic time.

Elizabeth didn't just need my therapeutic functions as a selfobject or empathic, regulating other—though of course she did need those functions. She needed *me*, Steve Stern, to be *her person*—the closest thing to a parent or primary attachment figure she would ever have. What does it mean to be there for the patient in the real way she actually needs, in order first to survive, then to come psychically alive—knowing there are always real limits to our availability and to the kinds of "realness" we can allow to develop and be actualized? During the first decade of our work together, I chose to make myself available, more or less as needed, for between-session phone contact. But one of the reasons I chose to do that was that I *was able* to without feeling overly burdened or resentful. I was still a bachelor and remained so until 1988, five years after Elizabeth's move to Chicago and our deep dive into analysis. So I had the time to give her. And we made it just under the wire! By 1988, Elizabeth had internalized our selfobject connection and function just enough to withstand the frustration of my gradually diminishing availability. As a marker of this growth, the self-induced vomiting she had used since age three to manage her overwhelmed states had pretty much dropped out by then. Newman had been right.

My marriage, and Elizabeth's growth, brought us into a different phase of our relationship, but the core issues and conundrums regarding the realness of the relationship remained central throughout the 40 years. Elizabeth's and my navigation of these conundrums required analytic perspectives that go beyond what I learned from Newman. Some of this thinking comes from Pizer's (1998) complex appreciation of the centrality of paradox in the deepest analytic engagements. What I would say about Elizabeth and me is that our good-enough engagement of these conundrums required a kind of unconscious collaboration wherein the real and the symbolic interact in complex, paradoxical, reverberating ways.

Because of the attachment security she gradually came to feel with me, and the progressive "fittedness" (Sander, 2008), or "specificity" (Bacal with Carlton, 2011), of our ability to process and meet her complex mental states across the full emotional range, Elizabeth, and we together, were able to reconstitute her sense of self based on repeated experiences (again using Sander's language) of "knowing herself as she is known." But the complicated question is: known by whom? What position did I have to occupy to exert this transforming influence? Elizabeth was very aware, often painfully, that our relationship meant something different to her than it did to me. But she needed it to mean something more to me than just being one among many patients—she needed to feel *met*, not only empathically and therapeutically, but in the realness and mutuality of our unique bond. At some point, maybe around our twentieth year, my reverie process came up with the word "thamily": We were each other's *thamily members*. I came to understand that, in a mutual analytic adoption such as ours, there needs to be a kind of *mutual claiming*, and a blurring of the line between the personal and the clinical in ways that do not threaten the essential boundaries and asymmetry of the analytic role relationship, nor obscure the fact that I could never become the equivalent of an actual parent.

To take one symbolic example, for many years I had resisted doing whatever it took to remember Elizabeth's birthday without her prompting me. I'm sure I was acting out a kind of analytic reality principle, as if I were saying: "No, I am not your real family member, and that needs to be okay." She always would say that she got it—that she knew it wasn't "right" or realistic for her to expect this. But in fact, she was always hurt by my not remembering. We both knew that as a child—the undeserving child—she only got a birthday celebration if the winter weather and her mother's mood allowed it. At some point something shifted and I realized: "What is my problem?! What possible harm could come from my making the effort to do this?" For the last decade of our work together I reliably remembered her birthday, calling her and leaving a message if we weren't meeting that day. And it was always extremely meaningful to her, even though it took 30 years of prompting *for me to finally get it*. Interestingly, doing this deepened something for me as well, expanding my own experience of our unique *thamily life*.

A Major Crisis Exposing the Dark Side of Analytic Adoption

There are certain inescapably painful paradoxes and conundrums inherent to the phenomenon of mutual analytic adoption. Elizabeth and I confronted our worst such crisis 20 years ago when I suddenly announced, after 25 years of working together, that I would be moving from Chicago to Maine and that this would be happening quite quickly. I should say that, caught up as I was in a somewhat impulsive, life-altering decision and transition, I was in a narcissistically preoccupied state at the very time I was informing all of my patients about my move. It is hard to convey the traumatic impact of this news. Elizabeth and I both understood that my physical presence in her life was part of what was life-saving for her, part of the "air" she had so desperately needed and had been "breathing" with me for decades. Thus, it was predictable and understandable that she felt deeply and personally abandoned and betrayed, both by the move itself, about which I had given her no advance warning, and the abrupt and less than fully empathic way I told her. As it turned out, I arranged my life so that I continued to see my Chicago patients in person every week for two years after the move, and once a month in person after that until the onset of the COVID-19 pandemic.

Despite these accommodations, Elizabeth remained in a state of hurt, frightened, enraged shock for years following my move. The move and the way I told her seemed heartlessly to negate and betray what she had experienced as a mutual commitment based on the progressive risks she and I both had taken over the years, gradually consolidating our mutual analytic adoption. She reminded me often that she had asked me if I was ever planning to move, and I, not knowing if I ever really would, said I had no such plans. I had known and anticipated the effect such a move would have on Elizabeth, and as testament to the mutual analytic adoption that *had* taken place, she was a significant factor in my deliberations about whether to move. I finally decided that, in the end, not moving because of Elizabeth would cause me to resent her. I shared all of this with her. She nonetheless remained profoundly sad and disrupted for years following my move. Elizabeth, who had always been good at coming up with metaphors that graphically captured her emotional state, said she felt as if she were sleeping in a cold room, and I had taken away a warm comforter, leaving her with only a thin sheet, shivering. In fact, during this period she often would lie on the floor at home, by herself, crying.

She "hated" the phone and said it was so much less than in-person meetings for her that she wondered whether to continue. We both understood how crucial my physical, bodily presence had been to the affect-regulation and sense of safety that were core elements of our relationship. There was a period when she reduced her session frequency, saying that the therapy had become so much less engaged and substantial due to the limitations of phone sessions that fewer sessions would be sufficient. She brought up the analogy of a divorced parent who moves away. Would the phone even come close to providing what a child in that position needed from that parent? I of course understood and agreed with her. This helped, but it didn't fundamentally change Elizabeth's traumatized response.

At the core of this crisis was the reality that, no matter how real and life-saving Elizabeth's and my mutual *analytic* adoption was, it was not the same as a familial bond; I was moving for and with my family, leaving her behind. This is a complex and charged reality that, almost inescapably, arises in some form in cases of analytic adoption. Even as Elizabeth felt betrayed and abandoned, her "adult" and "child" selves were in an intense struggle about my move. She understood at one level that she was not part of my family, and I was doing something I needed and had the right to do. Thus, she felt genuinely guilty about her angry, emotionally unraveled state, and worried I would lose patience, get fed up, and disengage. There was also the fact that because there *had* been a mutual analytic adoption between us, transferring to another therapist was unthinkable. We were supposed to be "thamily" to each other. Yet here I was, her person, her "thamily member," now abandoning her. All of this caused Elizabeth to feel deeply confused and panicked about who I really was to her and who she was to me.

In the end we did work through this crisis, and our analytic adoption not only remained intact; it was strengthened. There were a number of factors that contributed to this outcome. First was Elizabeth's staying power—her decision and determination to hang in there even at her most despairing. Second was my patience with and understanding of her anger, hurt, fears, and experience of betrayal, and her strong feelings about the diminished quality of phone therapy. Even after five years, I was fully accepting and tolerant of these feelings. Third was that she could sense my genuine guilt and sorrow about doing this to her, and felt I really understood its meaning to her and effect on her. Fourth was my agreement that our situation was indeed like the divorced parent who moves away. But I argued with her that it mattered how that long-distance parent then related to the child and conveyed understanding of the impact of the move. Finally, it came out that one of Elizabeth's worst fears was "out of sight, out of mind"— i.e., she would become less important and less special to me given that I now had new in-person patients and she was left behind. I tried to reassure her in every way possible that this was not the case, and over time she came to believe and *feel* that I was telling the truth—she was just as important to me as she had ever been.

I know Elizabeth would add that in the end our working through the agonies of my move was a strengthening experience for her in certain respects. It ultimately made her trust me *more*, allowed her to be more understanding of me as a separate human being, gave her a new, more realistic understanding of the inevitability of change, and enhanced her confidence that she could cope with such change.

Rethinking Termination

It had been ten years since we emerged from the five-year crisis set in motion by my move. Elizabeth had grown, and grown stronger, beyond what even the most hopeful Winnicottian analyst might have predicted 40 years ago. And I had grown with her. It would be an understatement to say, as Winnicott said to Guntrip, that she had been good for me, even as I had been good for her.

She had gradually reduced the frequency of her weekly sessions from five to four to three to two, and then, beginning in 2018, to one session per week. While her capacity for self-regulation had improved 100% within the context of ongoing therapy, termination remained beyond reach. Part of the issue, we both understood, was *me*—who I had become to her. Given that I was the closest thing to a good parent she had ever had, why would she want to end our relationship? It seemed unfair to have to do what real adult children don't. But she was not my actual adult child, signified by the reality that she paid me a lot of money to talk to me. She could afford it but didn't feel right about paying for therapy if she didn't still need it.

This issue has many layers and reverberating conundrums. Psycho-analysis is a treatment which, though often long, is supposed to end. Even within the psychoanalytic world, it's not supposed to take 40 years or more. In American culture at large, such a long-term dependency is heavily stig-matized, especially given that you have to pay for it. Life-long participation in AA or a Buddhist meditation community are honorable, while life-long therapy is shameful. These cultural judgments were magnified for Elizabeth because her feelings, instilled in her by her parents, that she was worthless and undeserving, caused her to feel guilty about every dollar she ever spent, or planned to spend, on therapy. This relentless shame and guilt played havoc with how important it had been for her to accept and affirm her true self, which included her true need for therapy and for me. Our being able, together, to hold all of this and allow the paradoxes and conflicting needs to unfold without judgment or pressure had enabled Elizabeth to hold stead-ily to the course of her own slow growth. But now, the end was very much in sight, whether it came in the form of her intentional termination, or my retirement for voluntary or involuntary reasons. Though she went back and forth, as I did, it seemed increasingly clear that she would rather terminate on her own before circumstances forced the issue, and while I was still around to help her with the transition. Since her therapy had been a big part of her life's work, it was a profound matter of self-esteem and personal accomplishment that she be able to do that. But, in order to do it she needed to feel that our relationship, and the very real love we had for each other, wouldn't end with termination. And so, we talked about that: about what forms our particular "thamily life" would take going forward.

Taking the Plunge

In January 2019, after anticipating and discussing the details throughout 2018, Elizabeth transitioned from once-weekly to once-a-month sessions. She had thought through the various possible arrangements and decided that, at least initially, she would see me in person whenever I came to Chicago, the frequency of which was down to about six weekends (six months) per year; during the other six months we would arrange once-a-month phone sessions.

In the final months of 2018, she got increasingly in touch with the magnitude of this change, and how hard it would likely be for her. She was very aware of the depth of her dependency after all these years—in touch with both the enormous therapeutic yield of that dependency, and the enormity of the task of letting go of it. In a November session she acknowledged her "anger that it has to be this way," and wanted to talk about what our relationship would look like in the "post-phase." I told her that I imagined a "loose understanding" that she could contact me whenever she needed or wanted to: I trusted her to be "mindful of all of the factors involved." And I said I thought it was important that there be no "cut off." In this sense, the hermeneutic of trust, which had been so central to our relationship all along, would continue into the termination and post-termination phases.

During this period of anticipation Elizabeth was reviewing our whole long relationship. One memory that stood out was that for many years *after* the period when she actually was calling me multiple times a week, I had said, almost ritually, at the end of every session: "Call if you need to." This was, again, an instantiation of the hermeneutic of trust—a later iteration of the same principle Newman had understood. In this case, my saying "Call if you need to" and meaning it created a symbolic *and* real holding space and was one of the elements that caused her not to need to call very often! Elizabeth reminded me that she had always "worked hard not to abuse your availability and to respect your privacy." All of this, of course, was relevant to, and prompted by, the change that was coming.

In our last session of 2018 Elizabeth expressed feeling sad but also determined that this was what she needed and planned to do. She felt confident that she no longer needed weekly sessions and that it would therefore be wrong on many levels to continue with that level of therapy. But she wanted to talk more about what our relationship would look like moving into the future. In particular, she wanted to know not only what was possible once she was no longer talking to me regularly, but what my approach to our relationship would be once I retired. This topic had come up before, and I had been pondering it for a while. I realized now that, like Elizabeth, I didn't want our relationship to end with my retirement, assuming I was still mentally and physically healthy enough to interact with her. I told her I was open to having some kind of contact post-retirement, though I didn't know exactly what that would look like. I said I thought the role structure of our relationship would always at least have the vestiges of therapist-patient. Here, we were both trying to imagine forms of relating for which there was no template or precedent—imagining what form our unique "thamily life" might take in its final stages.

For the first five months of 2019 Elizabeth felt progressively over-whelmed, and to some degree surprised, by how hard the thin schedule of monthly meetings was for her. There were many days when she wasn't sure she was doing the right thing, and she struggled not to give in to her power-ful longing to be in contact—to have the (regulatory) balm that talking with me had *always* provided her. Part of the challenge was that terminating reg-ular therapy *was*, in itself, dysregulating; indeed, this problem had derailed all previous, premature efforts to curtail the frequency of her therapy. One of the complexities during this period was that she was finding that our in-person meetings were "wonderful" when they were happening but left her with such longing that they seemed to be making her adjustment to the new schedule more difficult; thus, she wondered if we should reduce their frequency. Another dimension of this new phase was how alone she felt in it. There was literally no one besides me whom she could talk to about what she was experiencing in a meaningful way—no one she could assume would understand the unique position she was in or be able to be usefully empathic and supportive. This realization reinforced her conviction that it was essential for her to go through this terrible loss while I was still around to help her with it.

By June 2019, she had the strong feeling that she was "not doing well," was clearly worried about it, and wanted my help in figuring out what to do. For the first time there was the feeling that this change might be too much and that she might need to rethink her decision. There was a grow-ing feeling of pressure around all of this that was familiar to me from times past when my answer would likely have been for Elizabeth to reach for the help she needed and not suffer unnecessarily. But this time my own (mostly unconscious) processing during the month between our May and June ses-sions led me to a different place. In our June phone session, I found myself saying: "I think we need to take a big step back." I went on:

> Though it's been extremely hard, you've been able to do it so far with-out breaking down and calling between sessions. Really, isn't this exactly what we would expect you might be feeling right around now? Perhaps you had unrealistic hopes and expectations of how hard this would be. It's a *very* difficult, painful withdrawal after forty years, but

maybe this is what grieving the loss of our relationship (as it has been) feels like. Maybe you should try to hang in there for now and see what happens over a longer period of time.

These words seemed to strike the right chord, and Elizabeth's instantly calmer state was palpable, even over the phone.

When we next spoke in July, she was in a completely different place. She said that my perspective had been exactly what she needed to hear, and things had been significantly easier since our June session. She felt calmer, expressed renewed confidence that she was doing the right thing, and was starting to think about talking less than once a month in the near future! In short, her termination plan seemed to be back on track, working as she had hoped.

* * *

Analytic adoption inherently involves a profound and prolonged experience of surrender and dependency. Both patient and therapist implicitly (and sometimes explicitly) know this and worry about its long-term implications. There is no way for this necessary dependency not to have a downside. But in my experience, with many patients who have needed a prolonged dependent immersion, the therapeutic yield of this immersion is a gradual strengthening of "the self" such that, if the process is allowed to run its full course, the patient may well come to a point where they need the analyst less and spontaneously move in the direction of separation and termination. This is essentially the theoretical narrative of developmentally oriented theorists like Kohut and Winnicott (and their more contemporary exponents, such as Newman), and I have found it to be extraordinarily useful, although even more so with the progressive contributions and modifications introduced by relational and intersubjective theorists.

There are patients whose treatments, for a variety of possible reasons, don't follow this narrative. In particular, there are some who have been sufficiently damaged as children that, though they benefit greatly from a needed experience of analytic adoption, their senses of self and personal agency, and their self-regulatory capacities, may never consolidate enough to make possible the move toward relative independence. Although Elizabeth and I could never be sure until it actually happened, she ultimately did reach a place of sufficient strength and consolidation to take the plunge. Paradoxically, I believe one of the reasons she was able to do it was that I did not need her to and would not have judged her to be a lesser person or patient for making a different choice.

Conclusion: Themes and Variations

No two analytic relationships are alike. A corollary of this premise is that any general principles pertaining to therapeutic action rarely stand up as truly general principles that can be applied in the majority of cases in ways similar to the theorist's use of them in the original clinical contexts in which they arose. Both of these statements are implied in the psychoanalytic application of nonlinear dynamic systems theory, specifically the principle of "autocatalysm," which asserts that the "agent of change" in a given case "emerges as a product and property of the relational system itself" (Coburn, 2014, Kindle Edition, Introduction: "Attitudes," Attitude 4). But then, to the extent that these statements are true, how *do* we hold and apply our theories and more circumscribed principles, such as the principles I have put forward in this chapter as being relevant to work with psychically homeless patients? I can't imagine working with any other patient in exactly the same way I did with Elizabeth; so how does the reader-clinician glean something from this paper that is useable with different patients in very different treatments? What is the right "level of abstraction" for abstracting from one clinical context to another?

For me, the mediating construct is that of "the needed relationship" (Stern, 2017). Our goal with every patient is to co-create a relationship, unique to that dyad, which is going to facilitate that patient's growth and movement toward their implicit therapeutic aims and goals, given their unique personality organization, and the unique interactive chemistry of the dyad over time. Within this needed-relationship frame our theories play an essential role. Our theories, as we have internalized and integrated them, provide a linguistic, explanatory, and operational (procedural) matrix that enables us to "locate" our patients and interact with them "analytically." Every major theory has its own ideas about how the mind works and what kinds of relational response or stance our patients in general most need from us, and the same is true on a smaller scale with more circumscribed theories. The problem is that most real patients are too complex to be comprehended by any single theory, and most analytic therapists have their own unique takes on, and integrations of, multiple theories. These realities imply that the application of psychoanalytic theory by a given therapist with a given patient remains, essentially and inescapably, a creative and co-creative process—a process of "creating psychoanalysis freshly with each patient in each session of the analysis" (Ogden, 2009, p. 2).

I believe, based on my clinical experience over many years, that the three principles I have enunciated for working with psychically homeless patients are likely to be useful with many such patients; but the unique complexity of each case means that their application must always be subordinated to the overarching principle of co-creating the unique relationship each patient needs and can use.

Notes

1 I am grateful to Peter Rudnytsky for bringing this quote to my attention after hearing me present an earlier version of this paper at the APsaA National Meeting in New York in February 2019. Severn's book, *The Discovery of the Self: A Study in Psychological Cure*, was first published in 1933, then went out of print until Peter rediscovered and edited it for the Relational Perspectives Book Series (New York: Routledge, 2017).

2 By "mutual analytic adoption" I do not imply a symmetrical relation in which the patient adopts the analyst in the same sense that the analyst "adopts" the patient. I mean that the analytic adoption of the patient by the analyst is a development that both parties come to want and seek. One might say, loosely, that the patient comes to "adopt" the therapist as an adoptive parental (transference) figure, even as the therapist comes to analytically adopt the patient.

References

Anderson, J.W. (2014). How D.W. Winnicott conducted psychoanalysis. *Psychoanalytic Psychology, 31*: 375–395.

Aron, L. (1991). The patient's experience of the analyst's subjectivity. *Psychoanalytic Dialogues, 1*: 29–51.

Atwood, G.E. (2012). *The abyss of madness.* New York, NY: Routledge.

Bacal, H.A. with Carlton, L. (2011). *The power of specificity in psychotherapy: When therapy works and when it doesn't.* New York, NY: Jason Aronson.

Bach, S. (2006). *Getting from here to there: Analytic love and analytic process.* Hillsdale, NJ: The Analytic Press.

Balint, M. (1968). *The basic fault.* London: Tavistock.

Bass, A. (2007). When the frame doesn't fit the picture. *Psychoanalytic Dialogues, 17*: 1–27.

Coburn, W.J. (2014). *Psychoanalytic complexity: Clinical attitudes for therapeutic change.* New York, NY and London: Routledge, Kindle Edition.

Corpt, E. (2011). *Clinical generosity: An attitude deeply embedded in contemporary self psychology*. Paper presented at the Annual Conference, International Association for Psychoanalytic Self Psychology. Los Angeles, CA.

Davies, J.M. (1994). Love in the afternoon: A relational consideration of desire and dread in the countertransference. *Psychoanalytic Dialogues, 4*: 153–170.

Fosshage, J.L. (2007). Searching for love and expecting rejection: Implicit and explicit dimensions in cocreating analytic change. *Psychoanalytic Inquiry, 27*: 326–347.

Frankel, J.B. (1993). Collusion and intimacy in the analytic relationship: Ferenczi's legacy. In L. Aron & A. Harris (Eds.), *The legacy of Sandor Ferenczi* (pp. 227–247). Hillsdale, NJ: Analytic Press.

Guntrip, H. (1975). My experience of analysis with Fairbairn and Winnicott— (How complete a result does psycho-analytic therapy achieve?) *International Review of Psycho-Analysis, 2,* 145–156.

Hoffman, I.Z. (1998), *Ritual and spontaneity in the psychoanalytic process: A dialectical-constructivist view.* Hillsdale, NJ: The Analytic Press.

Hoffman, I.Z. (2009). Therapeutic passion in the countertransference. *Psychoanalytic Dialogues, 19*: 617–637.

Kernberg, O. (1975). *Borderline conditions and pathological narcissism.* New York, NY: Jason Aronson.

Kohut, H. (1971). *The analysis of the self: A systematic approach to the psychoanalytic treatment of narcissistic personality disorders.* New York, NY: International Universities Press.

Kohut, H. (1977). *The restoration of the self.* New York, NY: International Universities Press.

Little, M. (1985). Winnicott working in areas where psychotic anxieties predominate: A personal record. *Free Associations, 3*: 9–42.

Mendelsohn, E. (2007). Analytic love: Possibilities and limitations. *Psychoanalytic Inquiry, 27*: 219–245.

Newman, K.M., Kligerman, C., & Terman, D.M. (1988). Countertransference: Its role in facilitating the use of the object. *Annual of Psychoanalysis, 16*: 251–276.

Ogden, T.H. (2009). *Rediscovering psychoanalysis: Thinking and dreaming, learning and forgetting.* East Sussex, UK and New York, NY: Routledge.

Orange, D.M. (1995). *Emotional understanding: Studies in psychoanalytic epistemology.* New York, NY: Guilford Press.

Orange, D.M. (2011). *The suffering stranger.* New York, NY and London: Routledge.

Orange, D.M. (2012). *Development and response to the other: Engagement and enactment as bridging concepts among contemporary psychoanalytic groups.* Unpublished paper given at St. Paul University, Ottawa, April 20, 2012.

Pizer, S.A. (1998). *Building bridges: The negotiation of paradox in psychoanalysis.* Hillsdale, NJ: The Analytic Press.

Pizer, S.A. (2008). The shock of recognition: What my grandfather taught me about psychoanalytic process. *International Journal of Psychoanalytic Self Psychology*, *3*: 287–303.

Pizer, S.A. (2014). The analyst's generous involvement: Recognition and the "tension of tenderness." *Psychoanalytic Dialogues*, *22*: 1–13.

Sander, L.W. (1995). Identity and the experience of specificity in the experience of recognition: Commentary on Seligman and Shanok. *Psychoanalytic Dialogues*, *5*: 579–593.

Sander, L.W. (2008). *Living systems, evolving consciousness, and the emerging person: A selection of papers from the life work of Louis Sander* (G. Amadei & I. Bianchi, Eds.). New York, NY and London: Routledge.

Severn, E. (1933/2017). *The discovery of the self: A study in psychological cure* (P.L. Rudnystsky, Ed.). New York, NY: Routledge.

Shaw, D. (2014). *Traumatic narcissism: Relational systems of subjugation.* New York, NY: Routledge.

Slavin, J.H. (2007). The imprisonment and liberation of love: The dangers and possibilities of love in the psychoanalytic relationship. *Psychoanalytic Inquiry*, *27*: 197–218.

Stern, S. (2011). The therapeutic action of analytic love: Discussion of Joye Weisel-Barth's "Katherine: A long hard case." *International Journal of Psychoanalytic Self Psychology*, *6*: 489–504.

Stern, S. (2017). *Needed relationships and psychoanalytic healing: A holistic relational perspective on the therapeutic process.* London and New York, NY: Routledge.

Stolorow, R.D. (2006). Autobiographical and theoretical reflections on the "ontological unconscious." *Contemporary Psychoanalysis*, *42*: 233–241.

Stolorow, R.D. (2014). Undergoing the situation: Emotional dwelling I is more that empathic understanding. *International Journal of Psychoanalytic Self Psychology*, *9*: 80–83.

Weisel-Barth, J. (2011). Katherine: A long, hard case. *International Journal of Psychoanalytic Self Psychology*, *6*: 444–468.

Winnicott, D.W. (1962). The aims of psycho-analytic treatment. In D.W. Winnicott (Ed.), *The maturational processes and the facilitating environment* (pp. 166–178). New York, NY: International Universities Press.

Winnicott, D.W. (1965). *The maturational processes and the facilitating environment.* New York, NY: International Universities Press.

Chapter 6

On Management

The Art of Relating to Difficult Parents and Other Family-of-Origin Members

In my experiences working with adult children of negating parents, whether in individual or couples therapy, I have found that most want to maintain some kind of relationship with their family-of-origin members; and many still wish that things might get better such that they would finally receive at least some hint of the recognition they rarely, if ever experienced with their parents as children. I understand these longings, as I believe that adult children continue to need their parents *as parents* well into their adult lives. We don't need them in the same ways we did as children. But we want to feel that they are still there for us, that they love us more or less uncondi- tionally, that they would be available if we needed them in some reasonable way, and that we remain special to them. Even for those who did not feel these things from their parents as children, their needs are still present. If anything, they are stronger because of the leftover longings for the parents they never really had to begin with.

The problem is that both the wish to maintain a positive connection with one's parents and the need for them to still be parents in certain ways often run into the harsh reality that parents who did not do a particularly good job of meeting their children's emotional needs when they were young are unlikely to be able to do so with their adult children. Unless a parent has recognized their struggles and shortcomings as a parent and undertaken serious efforts to change, for example through their own therapy, it is unlikely that they will be capable of much more with their children simply because they became adults. There are exceptions to this rule, sometimes of a dramatic nature. A fictional example occurs in the popular TV series set in post-WWII Australia, *A Place to Call Home*. When the severe, ruth- lessly controlling matriarch of the Bligh family, Elizabeth, comes to see the error of her harsh, traditional attitudes, given the destructiveness they have

DOI: 10.4324/9781003585237-7

wrought with her children, she evolves into an openly caring, remorseful, unconditionally supportive mother. But such transformations are unusual in real life, which calls into service the idea of management.

Management is my word for a kind of relating to one's parents (and sometimes adult siblings) that takes into account the other's limitations while protecting oneself from frustrating, hurtful, often destructively escalating interactions. The principles are straightforward but putting them consistently into practice is more easily said than done. It requires practice, trial and error, and (initially) therapeutic support. Such support is especially indicated when the parents have been so traumatically negating of, or unengaged with, their child throughout development that almost any interaction with them can feel re-traumatizing. Introducing the concept of management can help patients: (1) face the reality of what their parents are and are not capable of; (2) set the stage for a necessary grieving process—grieving the reality of what they never had and probably never will have with their parents; and (3) align their expectations and behavior with these difficult-to-accept realities such that their interactions with their family members are as positive as possible. One might think of management as a form of *self-care* specific to one's relationships, as an adult, with difficult family-of-origin members. It can also be helpful with a difficult boss or any "complicated" person with whom one has to interact, or on whom one depends in certain ways.

For those who have been traumatized by poor early parenting, one of the projects of therapy is figuring out what kind of relationship, if any, one still wants with one's parents, and what kind of relationship is possible, given the parents' limitations and all that is stirred up emotionally in the patient when interacting with them. Many such patients begin therapy still caught up in repetitive patterns of hope, re-traumatization, and disappointment with their parents, and may spend many sessions bringing painful encounters to the therapist for help unpacking what is happening to them in these interactions and why they so often end up feeling undone, helpless, and either depressed or enraged, or both. (See, for example, the case of "Liz" in Chapter 1.) From an airless worlds perspective, it is often the case that in the early stages of treatment the patient's mind is still (in part) occupied and controlled by one or both parents (as they have been introjected over time) such that the patient is not yet sufficiently separated from them to know or claim their own true feelings and desires in relation to them. In such patients' minds, the parents are still watching and judging everything they say and do, and they still live in the grip of the parents' negating/controlling influence. For these reasons, it may be hard for the patient, in the early stages of therapy, to imagine a different kind of relationship with their parents—one in which it is possible to exercise more choice and control over how these interactions go.

When introduced at the right time and in the right way, the concept of, and skills involved in, management can help patients begin to see that there is an alternative to the relational patterns they have been stuck in with their parents. The point of analytic treatment is not to get patients to turn away from their parents (although turning away can be appropriate in extreme situations), but rather to help them figure out how to have a relationship with their parents that works for them. This means getting to a place where they are able to maintain a positive-enough connection, while, if possible, finding ways to express love and care without setting themselves up for disappointment and re-traumatization. Even with parents who have been traumatically neglectful, abusive, or negating throughout a patient's childhood, the adult child may feel a strong sense of moral/ethical responsibility toward them simply because they are their parents. ("Honor thy father and mother!") The principles involved in management provide a framework for incorporating such values, but doing so in a way that is realistic regarding how one's parents may or may not appreciate or reciprocate such loving impulses and actions.

Differentiating Management from Collaborative Dialogue

The catch is that in order to authentically and effectively make the shift to a management approach, one has to reach the point of giving up on one's parents in a certain sense. One needs to face the reality that one's parents may never be able to be the true parents one still hopes for—parents who recognize one's feelings and needs, respect one's perspective on things, and express awareness of, and remorse for, ways they have been hurtful in the past and perhaps continue to be so in the present. The shorthand for this group of capacities is the more general *capacity to recognize the other's subjectivity* (Winnicott, 1965; Kohut, 1971; Sander, 2002, 2008; Benjamin, 2002, 2004, 2018). (See also Chapter 4.) It is by dint of this capacity that a parent (or anyone, for that matter) is able to engage in *collaborative dialogue* (Lyons-Ruth, 1999) with another person. Adult children of negating parents run into trouble when they continue to hope for this all-important set of capacities in their parent(s). It is precisely in this situation that the idea of management becomes relevant; but it requires a shift within the adult child for it to become a useable strategy.

One can see these capacities being demonstrated very early in videotapes of mothers interacting with their five-month-old infants—infants who will go on to become securely attached to their mothers at 12 months (Beebe & Lachmann, 2014). Mothers with this capacity pay close attention to the baby's moment-to-moment expressions, movements, and overall communications, and they take these communications into account in their responses to, and initiatives with, the child during structured play conditions. One sees evidence of it, for example, when a baby shows signs of being distressed by something the mother has done, and the mother quickly moves to repair the disruption by stopping what she was doing and trying something different that is more attuned to what her infant will like. Moreover, infant researchers have long recognized that this is a two-way street. At the same time that mothers are getting to know their babies and figuring out how to be with them, babies are also getting to know their mothers as they learn (at a procedural level) how their mothers respond to them when they are expressing different things (needs, feeling states, reactions, initiatives, etc.). Citing Lyons-Ruth (1999, 2008), Beebe and Lachmann describe

> this process of coming to know and be known by another's mind [as] dependent on whether the partner (mother) is *capable of collaborative dialogue*. Collaborative dialogue involves close attention to the other's initiatives, openness to the other's state across the entire range of positive to negative emotions, attempts to comprehend the state or subjective reality of the other, the attempt to respond in a way that acknowledges or elaborates on that state, ability to negotiate similarity and difference, and efforts to repair disruption. Collaborative dialogues generate internal models in which both partners are represented as open to the experience of the other; each can know and be known by the partner's mind.
> (2014, p. 35; emphasis added)

By contrast, mothers who lack this capacity for collaborative dialogue—the capacity to attune to and meet the baby's spontaneous states, gestures, and needs, including the effort to repair ruptures and mis-attunements when they occur—tend to create conditions that lead to the child being insecurely attached at 12 months. Again, citing Lyons-Ruth (1999), Beebe and Lachmann write of this group that their

> dialogues involve a collapse of intersubjective space in which only one person's subjective reality is recognized. The partner's initiatives are ignored, over-ridden, or not acknowledged...such failures of collaborative dialogue generate contradictory internal models, in which the partner represents both roles, such as, "I should accept your control; I should attempt to control you."
>
> (2014, p. 36)

If we now fast-forward to the relationships between adult children and their parents, this same capacity for collaborative dialogue, or intersubjective relating, on the part of parents is still as central to the quality of their interactions as it was in infancy and childhood; though, of course, it takes different forms in adult life. Most interaction is now mediated by language and carries with it the cumulative residues (for both parties) of a lifetime of interaction and interactional *expectancies* generated by that relational history. Returning to my main point in this section: In my experience, parents who were seriously compromised in their abilities to recognize and meet their children's subjective realities and needs when they were young are unlikely to be much better at doing so simply because their children are now adults. Of course, as noted, there are always exceptions—some parents do change. Moreover, some parents are complicated in this regard: They may be able to recognize and meet their children in some ways and in some areas, but not in others. And those areas may be different with their adult children than they were when their children were young. As I sometimes say to patients, it is always an empirical question what their parents are capable of at this point in their lives.

The challenge for adult children of parents who (for the most part) lack this capacity for mutual recognition is the difficulty accepting that their parent(s) may never be able to engage in the kind of recognizing dialogue that they still, consciously and unconsciously, long for. And this hope affects the way they enter interactions with their parent(s) and other family members, and consequently how those interactions tend to go.

Kyle

This was the case in the early years of my work with Kyle—a happily married man in his 40s, with three elementary-school-aged children. Kyle grew up in a wealthy but broken family. Though I would not describe either of Kyle's parents as "traumatizing narcissists" in the full-blown sense that Shaw (2014) has illuminated, both were disturbingly narcissistic in their inabilities to transcend their own self-focused needs and recognize the emotional and developmental needs of their two sons. Their marriage had been stormy and hateful, due in part to a failed sexual relationship and the father's infidelities, and they had gone through an ugly, contentious divorce when Kyle was two. From ages 2 through 12 he, along with his younger brother, had required visits with the father on selected weekends, but these visits were never positive. From the time Kyle can remember, his father was focused on his own social world and needs, and was frequently gone, or present but preoccupied, during the sons' visits, leaving them to entertain and fend for themselves. Kyle, who was the more confident, assertive spokesperson for the two brothers, would complain to the father and beseech him to do fun things with them. The father once replied: "What do you want me to do, take you to Disneyland all the time?" Finally, at age 12, Kyle had grown so angry at his father's selfish neglect that he told his mother he didn't want to go there anymore. On hearing this, his father apparently said: "Ok, have it their way: We won't keep meeting at all." That essentially ended Kyle's relationship with him between ages 12 and 37, when he finally decided to reach out so that his children might have some relationship with their grandfather.

Things at home with his mother were better, but not by much. She was the more responsible parent in the sense of providing a stable home structure: "I at least always knew she was there." But she was developmentally arrested in her parenting capacities—incapable of setting aside her own needs and emotional reactivity in the service of her children's needs and development. She was socially insecure and had no real friends, only those she could buy with her wealth through charitable giving and favors such as letting people use her expensive seats at athletic events. Of her two sons, she favored Kyle because of his precocious ability to tune in to her needs. Indeed, she idealized him (perhaps as an unconscious husband-replacement) and unconsciously looked to him to take care of her in certain ways. Kyle had always thought of his mother's narcissistic attachment to him as love, and in a sense it was—or at least it was more than he got from his father. But he also came to understand that she could not tolerate interpersonal tension such as a child needing or demanding something of her emotionally, and she spent much of her time retreating to her bedroom and locking the door. This left Kyle and his brother physically alone much of the time, and emotionally alone all of the time. Thus, although Kyle grew up with the security and stability of enormous privilege, he, like Elizabeth in Chapter 5, who had grown up in a poor, working-class family, was essentially an emotional orphan, having to rely on his own resources to chart his path through adolescence and young adulthood.

In therapy Kyle emerged as a complex figure—likeable, engaging, competent in many ways, and open to our developing relationship, which he knew he needed. At the same time, he was skeptical of just how psychotherapy could help him beyond what he was able to figure out through his own self-scrutiny and change efforts. It slowly became clear that much of his adult adaptation and behavior were unconsciously motivated by what he had needed but never received as a child. In the absence of unconditional love, attentive care, role models he could idealize, and meaningful collaborative dialogue with either parent, he compensated by seeking recognition and validation for his talents and efforts through sports, academic achievement, and his natural leadership abilities.

At the stage in his life that I was getting to know him, he had practiced as a family lawyer for a decade, but ultimately decided he didn't like it because of the constant exposure to people's irresponsible behaviors, especially as parents. He also became disillusioned with what he perceived to be the amoral pragmatism of the legal profession: The game was more about winning than truth or justice. Indeed, irresponsible, self-centered behavior by anyone triggered Kyle's harsh judgment and anger bordering on rage. Targets for this judgmental rage included his parents, his brother, people he interacted with in work situations, his children (when they were defiant or being irresponsible, according to his standards), and himself (when he felt he wasn't living up to his own high standards). He didn't like this propensity for anger, and he would resolve to do better at controlling it, especially with his children. But these conscious efforts rarely held up when he was confronted by the other's disappointing behavior.

It also slowly emerged that alongside, or underneath, his anger was a life-long depression that took the form of a listless, unmotivated, helpless state, especially during periods when he had no work or other activities structuring his time and energy. Because of his family wealth, once he stopped practicing law, he had the luxury of not having to work at something he didn't enjoy. But he was having a hard time finding a career direction he was motivated to pursue. This left him with much unstructured time and persistent guilt feelings for not being more productive and engaged in work that the world would regard as laudable. During such periods he would lapse into a depressed, paralyzed state, which I came to understand as the depression resulting from the lack of any attentive care and involvement from either parent—an incapacity on either of their parts to recognize their children's needs and put them ahead of their own. This left Kyle in a chronically neglected, under-responded-to state, causing a low-grade depression from which there was no real escape. Using the word in a different sense, we could say that Kyle learned to "manage" or temporarily escape his depression through activities such as sports (at which he excelled), work, going to music concerts, and moderate drinking.

My understanding of the original and underlying cause of his depression prompted me, about a year into our work, to share with him Winnicott's (1967/1971) precept capturing a child's most fundamental existential need: "When I look I am seen, so I exist." Unexpectedly, my sharing this cracked open Kyle's ability to mentalize his primary childhood trauma for the first time, such that his engagement with, and belief in the potential of, psychotherapy dramatically deepened: "That's the most important thing anyone has ever said to me!" Someone had named and validated the actual situation of his childhood, which he had been trying to fight against and manage for his entire life up to that point. He reflected that what he saw as a child when he looked into his mother's eyes were *her* needs, not his true self. So, he was left *having to do things*—first for his mother and now for others—to get reactions that made him feel like he existed.

The Need for Management

From early in our work, Kyle reported his frustrations with all three other members of his family of origin: his mother, father, and brother. His issues with each of them were somewhat different, though all reflected the deprivations and dysfunction of his family growing up.

His most frequently reported struggle was with his mother. The family wealth had come from her side of the family, and she used it to create a very comfortable lifestyle. Her primary home was in the state where Kyle had grown up, but she now owned a second home in Maine which she had purchased in order to be able to be near her son's family during part of the year. Kyle had welcomed her arrival in Maine with extreme ambivalence. He wanted his children to have relationships with his family-of-origin members, but his mother's unilateral move into his adult world was problematic from the beginning. Though she wanted to feel like, and have Kyle and his family appreciate her as, a good mother and grandmother, she could never escape the prison of her own narcissistic needs, anxieties, and limitations, or her controlling, guilt-inducing ways of making sure those needs were met and her anxieties assuaged.

At the outset of treatment these narcissistic aspects of her character and presence were extremely problematic for Kyle. At one level (his adult self) he could see her limitations for what they were. But at another level (his child self) he could not accept that she could not change and do better and remained hopeful that, either through trying to placate her or attempting to engage her in direct conversations about her unacceptably selfish, manipulative behaviors, he would finally get through to her and have something like a real mother. These hopes set him up for repeated disappointments which left him in states of extreme frustration, anger, and depression, and often led to passive-aggressive withdrawals and standoffs that he hoped would induce his mother to see and acknowledge the effects of her behavior. But no matter what he tried, it never worked because she lacked the all-important capacities for mutual recognition and collaborative dialogue. In her conscious and unconscious psyche, Kyle was the one who was supposed to take care of her, and any generosity on her part was essentially transactional, entitling her to his doing whatever she needed from him.

Here's a typical example: At major holiday celebrations such as Christmas and family birthdays, his mother would insist that they have a separate celebration with her that did not include Kyle's wife Chloe's parents. Generally insecure in social situations with peers, Kyle's mother could not tolerate being together with Chloe's side of the family because she felt Chloe's parents tended to dominate. Really what that meant was that Chloe's parents were much more engaged with, and preferred by, Kyle and Chloe's kids than Kyle's mother. This was true for the simple reason that Chloe's parents enjoyed being and interacting with their grandchildren much more than Kyle's mother, who could not be bothered to play with them or show any sustained interest. Children of course feel these differences and act accordingly. This was a no-win situation for Kyle because, on the one hand, he resented indulging his mother's neurotic, unacceptable demands, but on the other had great difficulty tolerating her passive-aggressive, punitive withdrawal if he failed to comply.

It was such struggles with his mother (and with himself in relation to his mother) that prompted me to introduce the idea of management. I told him there was a different way of being with his mother that I called "management"—management, as opposed to true dialogue, of which his mother was incapable; but it would require being realistic about accepting that she likely could never be the mother he needed her to be. It would mean coming to terms with the reality that she was unlikely to change and that that would entail a kind of grieving on his part. Because Kyle is both smart and psychologically minded, he got this and quickly determined that this is what he would try to do. But I knew, and he saw before long, that this was more easily said than done.

Management and the Needed Relationship

In what follows I describe the complex processes in the evolution of our relationship over a decade of work, which led Kyle to become better able to skillfully manage his relationships with his mother, father, and brother. These skills in turn generalized to other non-familial relationships such as various work contexts in which his unconscious needs and hopes for love and recognition were activated along with the angry and depressive affects that emerged when those hopes were frustrated. As in my other analytic writing in the past decade, I believe the central factor in my work with Kyle has been the *total needed relationship* (Stern, 2017) that developed between us over time. Thus, though there was much specific work and emphasis on his need to better manage these relationships, our work in this area was inseparable from the needed relationship as a whole that was evolving between us. Indeed, his ultimate successes in the area of management were only possible because of our simultaneous attention to his experience of me and our relationship, including the defenses we slowly identified against his full trust and surrender within it.

I would name four key elements or principles which only in combination, and through deepening processes in all four areas, made truly effective management possible:

Meeting. The first and most general of these is *meeting the patient wherever they are at a given point in time*. (See Winnicott, 1962; Sander, e.g., 2008; Stern, 2017, and Chapters 2 and 3 in this volume, for more general discussions of this principle.) Kyle's need to develop management skills stemmed from the fact that his parents never were able to meet him where *he* was or based on *his* needs. They could only relate through their needs. Thus, it was critical, as it is in any analytic treatment, that I be able to meet him where he was during any given session. Only through his experience of being well-enough met could our relationship become a "useable" (Winnicott, 1969; Newman, 1988) resource in his interactions with needed others in his life.

Grasp. Developing the skills of effective management requires that both analyst and patient acquire an increasingly clear and nuanced grasp of the nature of the parents' (and sometimes other family members') limitations and problematic personality organizations that make mutual recognition and collaborative dialogue impossible. Shaw (2014) similarly emphasizes the importance of such "psycho-educational" work with adult children of traumatizingly narcissistic parents. This can be a slow and tortuous process because we are dealing not only with the patient's adult self, which may be capable of intellectually grasping the parents' limitations and pathologies relatively quickly, but with their child self, which unconsciously cannot relinquish the need for the parents to be true parents and thus cannot sufficiently separate from them internally to stand apart and act on the basis of the reality of the parents' limitations. In my experience, this capacity to begin to separate internally from one's parents depends on the increasing useability of the therapeutic relationship as providing a new experience of parent-like attunement and care. We can never become parents to our patients, but together patient and therapist can co-create a real relationship that provides analogues of needed parental qualities, attitudes, and capacities.

Grieving. As a patient begins to come to terms with what they needed but never received from their parent(s), and recognizes that the parents will likely never be capable of meeting (even the adult versions of) those needs, this makes possible a necessary grieving process, or at least a significant beginning of such a process, which in a sense never fully ends. The precursors of such grieving are all the overwhelmingly painful affects that a patient still carries from the traumatic parental deprivations and abuses of their childhood: Affects such as unbearable longing, depression, anger, and anxieties of all kinds related to their specific circumstances as children. Initially, as these affects come to light, they are simply unbearable feelings that must be quieted or defended against in some way because the patient's child self is still frozen in time, unconsciously still too tied to the parent, and not yet capable of integrating these affects into a true grieving process. But we hope that, as the therapeutic process takes hold and deepens, the patient's unconscious attachment to their parent(s) will begin to loosen or "soften" as, with the analyst's help, their capacity to make sense of these ancient traumatizing affects will begin to render them more containable and useable as part of the necessary grieving process—grieving the loss of that which they never had.

Management. The capacity for effective management comes in the context of the movement of these other three processes as they evolve and take hold over time. The nature of the management skills a given patient develops is always specific to their particular family and situations, and a unique outgrowth of each therapeutic relationship and the personalities of both patient and therapist. The acquisition of such skills usually needs to be prompted by a kind of coaching or guidance from the therapist, which takes into account where the patient is in their potential receptivity to such ideas, as well as the therapist's insights into how best to interact with problematic family members, given the unique nature of the interactional dynamics between parent (or sibling) and adult child. Our profession has been leery of offering any such coaching, viewing it as a non-analytic, behavioral technique. However, in the context of my needed-relationship framework, I view coaching as often a needed and essential element in the patient's in-depth acquisition of essential management skills. (See also Gedo's, 1979, work incorporating "instruction in psychological skills" within an analytic framework.)

In the narrative that follows I try to capture this multi-dimensional approach to management.

Kyle's and My Management Story

My first major interpretation to Kyle came five months into our work. The session had begun, characteristically, with his saying he didn't know what to talk about, felt frustrated, on the spot, anxious. "I often feel this way, like I have to produce something. I can't stand silences in groups." He also spoke of not feeling fully present, of there being a barrier, feeling lost. I said, "Let's stay with that." He thought and said, "I can rarely open up to anyone—really only my wife when I'm in the right mood." He associated to "not remembering anything from my childhood…I have always thought of my childhood as a normal middle-class childhood." I then said: "You can't remember anything from your childhood because you weren't free to fully experience your childhood. You were too preoccupied with parents who weren't present with you. Your father was focused on himself, and your mother was locked in her room nursing her wounds. You were living in a tense war zone from two to twelve. There was no one there to experience you fully and help you become a self. You had to manage it all by yourself." As I said this, Kyle became visibly upset and tearful: "It makes me angry and sad. How could they do this? They were my parents. I lost my childhood." He then associated to the 2012 movie *Beasts of the Southern Wild*. "In the end the young girl loses her loving father, and I completely lost my shit, crying uncontrollably." This was the first time Kyle had let both me and himself see and feel the full agony of the now-largely-dissociated impact of the traumatizing conditions of his childhood homes.

I was slowly getting a picture of Kyle's childhood and current life, and the nature of his conscious and unconscious struggles. His maternal grandfather—the family patriarch and generator of his mother's family's wealth—lived nearby and emerged as the closest thing to an engaged parent he had as a child. This grandfather was a strict disciplinarian such that the young Kyle knew he "always had to behave." He also was all about hard work, success, and being the best, and was judgmental of people who lacked the necessary drive and discipline. As the adult family member who took the most interest in him, Kyle idealized him and internalized these values, including his harshly judgmental attitude toward anyone who did not live up to them. It was therefore not surprising that Kyle applied these same values and expectations with his own daughter and sons, with the same judgmental harshness he had experienced from his grandfather. From very young ages, when his children did not live up to his expectations or were defiant of his efforts to ensure they were both responsible and well-behaved, he would become angry and punitive with them. To his credit, he knew he was getting too angry and was likely damaging them, but he had no control over his harsh behavior. Thus, this became a problem for which he expressed a need for my help. He desperately wanted to be a good, nurturing parent, unlike his own, but his uncontrollable propensity for disappointment and anger was seriously compromising these intentions.

He knew he was losing control in this area and would resolve to do better at containing himself, but it never worked. Clearly, his level of judgment and anger with his children was coming from some very painful, unconsciously dependent place within him and would not yield to conscious efforts at self-discipline. Those feelings would have to fully emerge within our analytic field before any real therapeutic traction would be possible.

Another window into his feelings was the immobilizing depressions that would take over when he was sick or otherwise prevented from working and being active. He would descend into a state he described as depressed, lonely, worthless, and unmotivated. I interpreted this as the core emotional state of his childhood, and now his child self. I said that it seems to come online when he is less active, busy, and doing—i.e., the main coping mechanisms he has used to manage life-long depression. This hit him very hard, especially what it implied about his mother as a parent. He felt he had accepted dismissing his father but had thought of his mother as more of a parent, more loving.

A year into our work, after several sessions during which Kyle was complaining about his damned-if-he-did/damned-if-he-didn't situation with his mother and finding that nothing he was trying was making a difference, he desperately wondered what he could do about it—how could he change that? My immediate response (which I had been thinking for a while) was that that would only change if he came more often to therapy. He had been coming once a week for a year, and I had reached the conclusion that only by coming more could we access his deeper emotional self. I said he could not think his way to a different place. His response was to feel stunned and disheartened—like I was saying he was more broken than he thought. Yet he also could say that he sensed I was right. Though it took another year for Kyle to process this idea and commit to a second weekly session, once he was coming twice a week he came up with his first management strategy with his mother: Rather than feeling at the mercy of her guilt-inducing demands for attention and inclusion, he would reach out to her in a proactive, positive way and schedule regular times that worked for *him* to get together with her. Around this time, his mother complained to him that his kids liked their other grandparents better. He replied that that was because she was less present with them than Chloe's parents. She then shocked him by saying she knew she had not been a very nurturant parent with either Kyle or his brother.

As he allowed therapy to become more central, he could begin to feel "the emptiness, sadness, and simply seeing the awfulness of it all." He also was aware that, as these feelings welled up around the totality of his parents' failures to be there for him, "it feels too big." He was seeing more clearly that "no one did their job; so, I'm way sensitive to that. But therapy is helping me be more emotionally present, so maybe you're doing your job!" Two months later he could say he was "feeling less defended, more fluid, stronger, feeling the yield of this process. Things are making more sense. I feel less like a ball of emotion that I have no clue about." One can see from these developments that management has an inner and an outer face. Kyle's slowly developing grasp of, and capacity to mentalize, the realities of his childhood were part of the inner field of our work, which was possible only to the degree that he was experiencing me as different from his parents—especially my interest in his emotional life and invitation to bring it fully into our relationship. Only as he could experience me as an interested, caring, and competent other could he begin to tolerate, process, and grieve "the totality" of his childhood traumas. But this did not occur all at once.

By our third year I was able to see and name his orientation to the responses of others and his strivings to impress them through his efforts of various kinds, such as his leadership roles on the school board of the school his kids attended. I said this would never get him where he wants to be because it's all based on conditional love: He couldn't yet feel he's already good enough as he is. In the next session he said how powerful the previous day's session had felt to him: He felt very affected by it: "I know it's true." He said it was a relief to have it named, but it left him feeling helpless. I said there's a more positive way for me to say it: "I like you; I've liked you from our first session; and there's nothing you could say, do, accomplish, or learn that would make me like you any more." Hearing this, his jaw dropped, and he became tearful as the session was ending.

As we were beginning our fourth year of work, I had an insight regarding his struggle to find meaningful work and his self-recriminations because of this. I interpreted that he was still operating at a younger developmental level of orienting toward the needed other—someone who could see and recognize him so that he could finally "exist." I said his work right now was in his relationships, especially his relationship with me. He was left "speechless and shocked" by the impact of this idea.

In the next session, he seemed to regress into a thoroughly depressed, unmotivated place, remaining mostly quiet throughout the session. I observed and shared that he looked like a very unhappy kid, alone in his room, helpless to do anything that would help him feel better. I added that I also thought there was anger embedded in his self-accusations. He responded that he felt frustrated with himself for not seeing a way forward out of this depressed, paralyzed state. I interpreted this impulse toward action as a defense against his experience of not being seen or cared for by either parent, and his understandable anger, hurt, and depression about that. His association was that if he were back on the market, he couldn't get a woman to have sex with him.

A month later he was "in a different, calmer place"—not feeling as compelled toward the other: "I'm saying 'no' to things; I'm feeling a greater sense of confidence." He felt a grieving process was taking place vis-à-vis his mother and his childhood. He also felt he was managing his mother better—being more assertive with her without expecting any real change. But then, following a trip to his home state to visit his parents, he was left feeling angry at both of them: "Both of them are selfish, controlling, and guilt-inducing." His father had "insinuated himself on us" despite Kyle's efforts to limit their contact; and his mother had been "impossible," refusing to come to his older son's birthday party because Kyle's father and stepmother would be there. "I was the only adult in the room—the only one able to focus on what was important." I encouraged him to stay with these feelings rather than focusing on management. He got in touch with memories of feeling helpless as a child in the face of their selfish unpredictability. By the next day's session he was "in touch with sadness, anger and confusion." He realized that his kids created a need for something from his mother, which made him vulnerable because she couldn't do what he needed her to. And he now recognized that there would be no gain from punishing her or trying to get her to be capable of more. He felt "alone, angry, frustrated, depressed, and helpless—with no possibility of dialogue or justice!"

By the end of our fourth year of work, we were fully in the mid-phase of treatment. Kyle had grasped the core nature of his childhood traumas and was beginning to experience and grieve his overwhelming pain and anger in response to both parents' failures to be there for him in fundamental ways. Moreover, he was using our relationship—my presence and guidance—to manage both of these relationships better—that is, in ways that took their limitations into account and made him less vulnerable to the impossible binds they put him in and the suffering they caused. But, as I have come to understand these things, the crux of Kyle's problem with both inner and outer management was one of *separation*—the capacity to separate sufficiently from his parents *internally*, to act as his own agent in relation to them and grieve the deprivations and injuries that dominated his childhood and continued to haunt him. And the only way to achieve such separation was through his relationship with me—specifically by experiencing me as a real-enough other who, within the context and frame of psychoanalysis, co-created with him a unique form of needed attachment and care; or, in different language, co-created a "useable object" or selfobject relationship (Winnicott, 1969; Kohut, 1984; Newman et al., 1988).

In a session during this period Kyle said he was feeling less of a need to control things he can't control—for example with his kids. He was more accepting of people's limitations. But I wondered to myself whether he had internalized our relationship enough for that to hold. This was tested by an incident at home when their cat fell off a high shelf, bringing down some glasses with it. Kyle's first reaction was rage at his family for not protecting the cat, but then he judged himself for his rage. I suggested a more compassionate take: recognizing that his real rage was at those who had not taken care of *him*. I said that because his parents had not taken care of him, his inner resources for taking care of others were compromised, especially when they were being difficult or disappointing. He felt we were getting at the crux of something—"a most important truth." A few weeks later he reported being in a good place—feeling better at moderating his reactive anger. He also noted that he does better when he makes both of his weekly sessions. When he misses a session, he notices a "decay in the positive effects of coming here."

A month later, anticipating a trip to visit his father, he said he was seeing him more clearly: His father had never had his back such that he could truly trust and "fall back" on him. Instead, he has had to carry himself. He said he felt stuck with feelings he now understands but has no way to heal or resolve. I wondered out loud what that implied about our relationship. He reflected and said I carried a flashlight which I gave to him with occasional hints about where to shine it. In that way, I've enhanced his reflective capacity. I thought to myself: No, it's more than that; there's been some relational healing, but it hasn't gone all the way. I said I felt he was letting go and trusting me more, but was still pretty self-contained. He agreed.

In late 2019, Kyle was complaining about the executive board of a local non-profit community organization that had retained him as a consultant to their capital campaign. (He had previously and successfully led such campaigns for other organizations.) He was finding the board members to be both disengaged and obstructionist and had been struggling with alternating feelings of anger, helplessness, and apathetic withdrawal. The word that occurred to me at that point was *partners*. Like his father and mother, the board members had not been good partners in his work with them—they weren't doing their part. He found this idea illuminating and it put him in touch with old feelings. A week later he reported that a shift had occurred in his attitude toward the consultation. He decided he needed to "step up and dedicate myself to the time it really requires." He had concluded that they needed to hire a part-time support person for the campaign. This realization ushered in "a greater sense of calm, confidence, and peace—no longer looking to anyone for affirmation—more self-contained." This illustrates how a shift in his management capacities with this difficult group emerged not from any direct coaching but from our analytic connection and my "specificity of recognition" (Sander, 2008; Stern, 2017) of his experience with them.

In a session in January 2020, the beginning of our fifth year of treatment, Kyle expressed "a profound sense of things not mattering and arbitrariness," and of "not caring and not knowing what to do." He said he wasn't feeling in acute pain but knew this was a form of depression. I interpreted that he didn't feel "woven to the world" because both of his parents had failed to weave him to the world...to his future (Loewald, 1960). He started the next session in a "paralyzed, disconnected place, disconnected from myself and everyone." He didn't know what he wanted to do over the upcoming weekend and wished Chloe would just decide for him—whether to stay home or go skiing. I linked this state to where we had ended the previous session—he was "unwoven" to the world *and* himself and needed someone to step in and weave him to something. I said I could imagine him as a child in this state—suffering from emotional neglect and the failure of either parent to perform this active joining/weaving function. This resonated for him—he found it "very integrating." He said he always assumed there must be something wrong with *him*, so he has had to work to get people to love and help him. I said I didn't think there was anything wrong with him but there's a way that he keeps himself, understandably, half-connected and half-disconnected. He agreed and used as an example the state he was in at the beginning of the session. I considered this and said that, as far as I was concerned, that was a state that *connected* me to him because of his openness and vulnerability—it inspired me to engage and try to help him weave him to himself and his life. He expressed feeling surprised and pleased by that.

As COVID-19 was descending on all of us, Kyle was descending quickly into a depressed, apathetic state, anticipating what life would be like for him under total lockdown with his young adolescent children at home full-time. In his words, he didn't "even have a fantasy of someone coming to take care of me." This felt unnerving and concerning to me, especially as we were suddenly meeting remotely with technology glitches during sessions. I knew this was a potentially high-risk situation for Kyle—a prolonged period of social isolation with very little to do that would distract him from his depression or enable him to engage in performative activities with individuals and groups who would respond appreciatively. It was as if he were being plunged back into his parentless childhood with no relief in sight.

Then, as if "someone" had actually heard his desperate sense of panic, he was asked to be the board president of his children's school, and the person responsible for shepherding the school through the pandemic—what turned out to be a full-time volunteer position. He was thrilled to have been asked and happy to be on the job right away, with much to deal with, given the shutdown of in-person classes. He felt confident in his ability to perform in this role and very quickly reversed his plunge into depression.

This job turned out to be uncannily fortuitous because it offered Kyle and me many opportunities to deal with management challenges posed by parents who weren't *his* parents. Kyle rose to the occasion of this complex assignment, establishing scientifically informed policies affecting all aspects of school life, with different policies for children of different ages. But the very nature of the situation (with all parents being fiercely protective of their own children and no policy that didn't have complainers) placed Kyle at the center of the storm, having to deal constantly with people trying to pressure him, and becoming extremely displeased, even threatening, when he failed to comply. It was like basic training in management—but management at a

"middle distance" (Sullivan, 1956, p. 375; Gustafson, 1986, pp. 48–50)—
i.e., with other people's parents, not his own.

For example, in one session he was struggling with his susceptibility to
feeling guilty and bad about himself when school parents were displeased
when he didn't do something they wanted. He could step back and intellectually recognize that it was their problem, but this wasn't enough to counter
his sinking into a "helpless sense of badness and insecurity." I interpreted
the presence of his child self—a child who was profoundly affected by
whether the reflection coming back to him was "a gleam" or "a glare." This
led him to question why he was so stuck in the place of anger at his own
parents, epitomized by the question: "How could you have done this, been
this way, not done better, been so self-absorbed, not been a real parent?"
I said: "Your anger and sadness are appropriate, and it's hard to face the
fact that your parents can't really respond to you without doing more of the
same." I reflected that he felt alone with these feelings and "unmet entitle-
ments." I said: "The only way I know to help is through our relationship
which, hopefully, over time, will expand your experience of 'gleam' and
diminish the power of 'glare.'" He responded: "I think we just opened up a
whole new level of realization, but, of course, our time is up!"

By July 2020 Kyle was in "a very good, calm, confident place"—comfortable in his job of School Board President and pandemic manager. He
saw "real change and growth" in his not needing constant approval and
affirmation and was feeling "freer to be myself and find my own voice"—
feeling "more at peace" with realizing what he can and can't control. He
credited our work, saying he felt a new sense of "space" or "separation"
from others he had to interact with.

Things were improving, both with his ability to manage the tensions and
people at school and his interactions with his mother and father. However,
we were both aware that a core underlying depression—the legacy of his
parentless, alone state as a child—might be being masked by his busy-
ness and successes. Thus, it was not surprising that there were sessions he
began in a "claustrophobic, trapped, flattened, depressed place," and this
could prompt a sense of "futility." In one such session in March of 2021
he reported "desperately trying to do something that would help him feel
better"—but it wasn't working. His immediate family were each "caught
up in their own responsibilities and self-preoccupations" and his family
of origin were all "woefully lacking." It seemed to Kyle like nothing he

or we could do would make a difference in this depression—his sense of aloneness and desperation. I agreed and added that he and I seemed to be stuck in a pattern that was foreclosing any real change in this core area. I said the closest I could come to an explanation was that we tended to fall into a familiar "bro"-like pattern of conversation, which can't address the core needs fueling his depression. His response: "That's depressing!"

That session opened a door to focusing more intentionally on what was and wasn't happening in our relationship. The door remained open several months later, in May 2021, when I was giving him feedback that his management of things at school "showed some slippage to the degree that he was looking to them to meet his emotional needs, which they will never do." This opened up something for him—a clearer realization that I was right about that, which led immediately to the question: Then how does he get his need (to be taken care of) met? I answered: "I would think that comes back to our relationship—I'm curious about that."

His "gut reaction" was that that was too much to put on our relationship and that he didn't think of it in those terms. "Plus, I already do experience you in that way more than anyone else." In the following session he wanted to come back to this question of why he didn't/wouldn't allow me to be more in the position of providing the care he needs. His thought was that the thing he needs most is affirming praise from someone who really knows the process and capacities he's being praised for—like knowing the details of the job he's done as board chair. He assumed I was not tracking him in that way. I immediately questioned that, arguing that I did have enough data and felt I was very aware of how complex his job was and how good he was at it. I then wondered if that was the real problem: Wasn't it more likely that it's because he pays me as his therapist and thus can't really trust that I offer the equivalent of unconditional love? His immediate response was, "Then how do I get from point A to point B?"

In the following session he said that the previous session had been "important" and had left him "processing a lot." He was especially affected by what I had said about having more of a sense of his capacities than he had realized, in response to which he seemed genuinely surprised and moved. He also said he was struck by what I was saying about what he might be missing with me as someone who was taking care of him in a certain way. In language I introduced in Chapters 2 and 3, this exchange turned out to be an inflection point in the treatment, following which he began to more fully experience me as the "complex selfobject" he needed. There was a greater sense of relaxation and surrender, unlike anything he had experienced with either parent. There was now the feeling, at least as I was experiencing it, that we were "breathing together."

Though we did not explicitly come back to the topic of our relationship, it seemed significant, and not coincidental, that in the sessions immediately following, he opened up in a new way about his last significant management challenge: his deteriorating relationship with his brother, Andy. Kyle felt a deep kinship with Andy because they had lived through the same childhood deprivations together—the years of empty visitations with their father and their mother's narcissistic retreats to her locked bedroom. But their adaptations to these conditions were very different. Kyle was two years older and had clearly been the dominant brother. He was the one who angrily confronted their father, and he was the one their mother had idealized and looked to for some kind of caretaking. And outside the home, Kyle had been an over-achiever whereas Andy was a more passive, less motivated under-achiever. These tendencies had continued into adulthood. While Kyle moved out into the world and was successful in many ways, Andy still lived in close proximity to, and was more dependent on, their divorced parents. Though both brothers were married with children, Andy had never pursued a career and seemed content to live off his inherited wealth. Kyle felt judgmental toward his brother for this lack of ambition and productive work and had, with the best of intentions, tried to encourage him to do something more with his life. Not only did that not happen, Andy and his wife had gravitated toward a group of friends who were similarly wealthy, unambitious and content to focus on their own pleasures of various kinds. In this way, Andy was beginning to take after his father who, starting in mid-life, had become increasingly infatuated with Porsche automobiles such that the organized world of Porsche enthusiasts had become his primary identity and focus. If a Porsche convention conflicted with a planned visit to see Kyle and his family, either the Porsche convention won out, or it would be obvious he was missing the convention during his visit. During one such visit, Kyle gave him a t-shirt with the inscribed message: "I'd rather be at Porsche!"

In recent years Kyle had felt increasingly disappointed in, hurt by, and angry with his brother for his diminishing interest in connecting with him and his family in any meaningful way. The last thing they had done together was a serious mountain biking marathon/competition. This was mainly an interest of Andy's, and Kyle had trained for an entire year to prepare for the very challenging event, which had taken place in the early years of our therapy. But, since then, the pattern was that, while Andy seemed to express interest in getting together during Kyle's visits to his home state and family, when it came down to it, he was barely available and not at all thoughtful or active about planning encounters between their two families. Though Kyle could see that this was the direction things were going, he continued to feel hurt by, and angry at, Andy for his seeming rudeness and failure to take any responsibility for maintaining their relationship.

I had been trying to help Kyle think about this problem for some time, realizing it was a relationship that, increasingly, called for management of some kind as opposed to the more real fraternal dialogue the two brothers had had in the past. But Kyle was, for understandable reasons, having difficulty fully accepting this change. As a more dispassionate observer of Andy through Kyle's reports, I had been forming my own picture of him and the direction in which his life seemed to be moving. I told Kyle I thought his brother meant it when he said he wanted to get together. But when it came down to it, he couldn't follow through. I said my sense was that Andy had a very different experience of their relationship than Kyle. He had always been living in Kyle's shadow and knew that Kyle had always been the mother's favorite. And because Kyle had been judgmental of Andy for his lifestyle, Andy probably felt more conflicted about their relationship than Kyle did. Meanwhile, Andy seemed drawn toward an increasingly limited, narcissistic world of people with similar means, values, and interests, such that within that world he didn't feel bad about himself. Their shared bike race had been a good choice of activity because it had taken place in Andy's world and had been initiated by Andy. This all started to make sense to Kyle and "hit" him "in a new way."

I went on to say I thought the implication for management was that Kyle might need to approach their encounters differently. Mainly, he needed to be more accepting and less judgmental of Andy's choices. And rather than adopting his usual take-charge approach, making plans far in advance, including all the restaurant reservations, I suggested he try a more laid back stance and let Andy be the one to decide what they would do, at least some of the time, all the while being prepared for the possibility that nothing would happen or something would be organized only at the last minute. Kyle got this and saw the logic: He felt he could, and agreed he needed to, make such a shift. In subsequent visits things did go better, but mainly because of Kyle's reduced expectations. Andy was somewhat more engaged, but it was hard for Kyle to tolerate it when Andy and his family did nothing for Kyle's younger son's birthday. However, Kyle was able to see more clearly his brother's "victimized, passive-resistant, unmotivated, disengaged" self-organization. The bottom line was that Kyle was learning to accept the loss of the relationship he had always hoped for with Andy, thus leaving him feeling even more alone in relation to his family of origin, but better able to manage his interactions with all of them.

Conclusion

As I write this, several years have passed. Kyle has settled into a more realistic place in relation to his family and is more comfortably managing all his interactions with them. This is not to say he is never triggered by their behaviors toward him and his family. But he has each of them—mother, father, and brother—in far better perspective. About a year ago I first mentioned that I was thinking of writing about him (and us). Surprisingly, he said he had actually thought about that possibility and even mentioned it to Chloe, whose reaction was that I "could write a whole book about him!" I told him I *was* writing a book and thinking of doing a chapter on the topic of management. He immediately got excited about how "useful and essential" our work on this had been—not just with his family but in his school job as well. He felt he had "gotten to a whole new level of being able to handle and keep in perspective anything, no matter how charged or angry, that comes at me."

I believe these changes were made possible not only through helping Kyle develop a new skill set for relating to significant people in his life but through the deepening of our relationship over time. Our discussions about our relationship in 2021 had marked a turning point, following which Kyle allowed himself to trust and "fall back on" *me* as someone who not only knew and understood him but who genuinely cared about him and the quality of his life.

References

Beebe, B., & Lachmann, F.M. (2014). *The origins of attachment: Infant research and adult treatment.* London: Routledge.

Benjamin, J. (2002). The rhythm of recognition: Comments on the work of Louis Sander. *Psychoanalytic Dialogues, 12*: 43–54.

Benjamin, J. (2004). Beyond doer and done to: An intersubjective view of thirdness. *Psychoanalytic Quarterly, 73*: 5–46.

Benjamin, J. (2018). *Beyond doer and done to: Recognition theory, intersubjectivity and the third.* New York, NY: Routledge.

Gedo, J.E. (1979). *Beyond interpretation: Toward a revised theory for psychoanalysis.* New York, NY: International Universities Press.

Gustafson, J.P. (1986). *The complex secret of brief psychotherapy.* New York, NY: W.W. Norton.

Kohut, H. (1971). *The analysis of the self: A systematic approach to the psychoanalytic treatment of narcissistic personality disorders.* New York, NY: International Universities Press.

Kohut, H. (1984). *How does analysis cure?* (A. Goldberg & P. Stepansky, Eds.). Chicago, IL: University of Chicago Press.

Loewald, H. (1960). On the therapeutic action of psychoanalysis. In *Papers on psychoanalysis* (pp. 221–256). New Haven, CT: Yale University Press.

Lyons-Ruth, K. (1999). The two-person unconscious: Intersubjective dialogue, enactive relational representation, and the emergence of new forms of relational organization. *Psychoanalytic Inquiry, 19*: 576–617.

Lyons-Ruth, K. (2008). Contributions of the mother-infant relationship to dissociative, borderline, and conduct symptoms in young adulthood. *Infant Mental Health Journal, 29*(3): 883–911.

Newman, K.M., Kligerman, C., & Terman, D.M. (1988). Countertransference: Its role in facilitating the use of the object. *Annual of Psychoanalysis, 16*: 251–276.

Sander, L. (2002). Thinking differently: Principles of process in living systems and the specificity of being known. *Psychoanalytic Dialogues, 12*: 11–42.

Sander, L. (2008). *Living systems, evolving consciousness, and the emerging person: A selection of papers from the life work of Louis Sander* (G. Amadei & I. Bianchi, Eds.). New York, NY and London: Routledge.

Shaw, D. (2014). *Traumatic narcissism: Relational systems of subjugation.* New York: Routledge

Stern, S. (2017). *Needed relationships and psychoanalytic healing: A holistic relational perspective on the* therapeutic process. New York, NY: Routledge.

Sullivan, H.S. (1956). *Clinical studies in psychiatry.* New York, NY: W.W. Norton.

Winnicott, D.W. (1960/1965). The theory of the parent-infant relationship. In D.W. Winnicott (Ed.), *The maturational processes and the facilitating environment* (pp. 37–55). New York, NY: International Universities Press.

Winnicott, D.W. (1967/1971). Mirror-role of mother and family in child development. In D.W. Winnicott (Ed.), *Playing and reality* (pp. 111–118). London: Tavistock. (Original work published 1967)

Winnicott, D.W. (1962). The aims of psycho-analytic treatment. In D.W. Winnicott (Ed.), *The Maturational processes and the facilitating environment* (pp. 166–178). New York, NY: International Universities Press.

Winnicott, D.W. (1969). The use of an object and relating through identifications. In D.W. Winnicott (Ed.), *Playing and reality* (pp. 86–94). London: Tavistock Publications.

Appendix

Theoretical Roots of "Identification with the Other's Response to the Self"

My concept of *identification with the other's response to the self* draws on the history of a certain kind of identification within psychoanalytic theory. The following is a brief summary of that history.

Identification was central to Freud's (1917, 1920, 1923) understanding of structure formation: Both the ego and the superego were understood to be formed largely from identifications arising from various stages of development. Laplanche and Pontalis (1967/1973) captured the significance of the concept for Freud when they wrote, "In Freud's work the concept of identification comes little by little to have the central importance which makes it, not simply one psychical mechanism among others, but the operation itself whereby the human subject is constituted" (p. 206). With the gradual shift from the structural model to developmental, self, and relational models, however, identification lost its theoretical anchor, leaving it one of the most relied upon but under-theorized concepts in contemporary psychoanalytic discourse.

A phenomenon akin to Freud's (1920, 1923) concept of "primary identification" remains implicitly central in many post-structural theories of the self and needs to be incorporated more explicitly into contemporary relational and intersubjective thinking. There is a sense of identification that emerges in the developmental models of Loewald (1960, 1978), Winnicott (e.g., 1967), Kohut (1971, 1977), Bollas (1987), Sander (1977, 1985, 1995), and Ogden (1994). It is identification as the basis for self-realization. To state the idea strongly, the child's experience of their inner reality does not become psychologically real to the child, and therefore fully useable, except through identification with the responses of significant others to their inner reality.

Loewald (1960), still working within the structural model, could comfortably use the word identification to describe this process:

> The child, by internalizing aspects of the parent, also internalizes the parent's image of the child—an image that is mediated to the child in the thousand different ways of being handled, bodily and emotionally. Early identification as part of ego development, built up through introjection of maternal aspects, includes introjection of the mother's image of the child. Part of what is introjected is the image of the child as seen, felt, smelled, heard, touched by the mother.
>
> (p. 229)

While no longer calling it identification, Ogden (1994) uses very similar language to describe the same phenomenon:

> When the mother is capable of reverie, she names (gives shape to) the infant's experience through her interpretation of the infant's internal states. For instance, the infant, in the beginning, does not experience hunger; he experiences a form of physiological tension that is not yet a psychological event that can be contained by the psyche of the infant alone. The mother's act of sensing the infant's tension, her holding him, looking at him, feeding him, talking and singing to him, all represent facets of an "interpretation" of the infant's experience. In these ways, hunger is created and the infant is created as an individual (i.e., the infant's raw sensory data are transformed into a psychologically meaningful event) through the mother's recognition of hunger.
>
> (pp. 46–47)

The young child has a primary inchoate experience of its ongoing existence, including its needs, tension states, sensations, affects, and interests. The mother, and ultimately both parents, respond to these expressions with more or less empathic recognition of the child's subjective experience, and the child's sense of self is formed accordingly. As Winnicott (1967), in his famous aphorism, characterized this process from the child's perspective: "When I look I am seen, so I exist" (p. 114). Loewald (1960) expressed a similar idea when he wrote, "the child begins to experience himself as a centered unit by being centered upon" (p. 230). As noted, of the different kinds of identification described by Freud (1917/1957, 1921/1955b,

1923/1961), the type implied in these various theories is an aspect of "primary identification" (Freud, 1921/1955b, 1923/1961; Fairbairn, 1952; Loewald, 1978/1980a)—identification of the pre-oedipal as opposed to the oedipal period—which Freud (1921/1955b) characterized as "the earliest expression of an emotional tie with another person" (p. 105).

Fairbairn (1952) defined primary identification as

> a process by virtue of which the individual fails to differentiate himself from, and thus spontaneously identifies himself emotionally with, those upon whom he emotionally depends. So intimate is the connection between identification and infantile dependence that, psychologically speaking, they must be treated as the same phenomenon.
>
> (p. 275)

Loewald (1973/1980b, 1978/1980a) also viewed primary identification as essentially synonymous with early relatedness and with development as it occurs within the mother-infant matrix. "Internalization," Loewald (1973/1980b) wrote, "is conceived as the basic way of functioning of the psyche, not as one of its functions" (p. 71). For Loewald, in the infant's nascent subjectivity there is as yet no differentiation between subject and object: The relationship is one of complete and inescapable identification. Moreover, development only proceeds through identificatory processes, that is, through internalization or appropriation of experiences of mutual recognition and attunement. Only through such felicitous identificatory experience, argued Loewald (1978/1980a), does the ego or self come into being as a psychologically differentiated entity. Like Freud, Fairbairn, and Loewald, I view identification as an intrinsic aspect of self-development.

Note that the type of identification involved in this early self-realization process is identification not simply as imitation but rather as appropriation of the total intersubjective experience, as apprehended by the child. (Seligman, 1999, has made a similar distinction.) I assume that this type of identification begins at birth, occurs initially as a presymbolic form of learning, and becomes part of what has variously been called the core self (Stern, 1985), the unthought known (Bollas, 1987), the prereflective unconscious (Stolorow and Atwood, 1992), and implicit relational knowledge (Stern et al., 1998). Bollas' (1987) concept of "the self as object" has been especially helpful in capturing the fact that part of this core experience of self is the tendency to experience and treat ourselves as we have been experienced and treated by our early objects.

Over time and repetition these early "procedural" identifications with others' responses to the self become increasingly consolidated organizers of the child's self or subjective world. This is essentially what Kohut (e.g., 1984) meant by transmuting internalization, except that he had no counterpart to account for structure formation under pathological conditions. Interestingly, Fairbairn (1952) had the opposite bias: He believed that internalization of object relations occurred *only* under pathogenic conditions, not under healthy ones. I believe, as Bollas' (1987) model suggests, that there is more symmetry here than either Kohut or Fairbairn allowed; that for the young child, identification with the other's response to the self is a constant, like breathing; that whatever the child's intersubjective experience with caretakers, he or she will identify with that experience.

An important characteristic of these early identifications is that, insofar as they are the primary way that a child comes to know themself, they are experienced as undifferentiated from the aspects of primary subjective experience that are associated with them (Loewald, 1978). When the identifications are with attuned or facilitating responses, this undifferentiated quality yields the sense of consolidation or cohesion described in self-psychological theory (Kohut, 1971, 1977). When parents fail to recognize their child's psychic reality and needs, the identifications that form alienate the child from that reality and disable his or her capacities to relate to the external object world on the basis of authentic self-experience. In this case, their undifferentiated quality creates the pathogenic paradox of their being simultaneously of the self and alien to the self—a quality first described by Ferenczi (1933), as a "confusion of tongues" and referred to by Fonagy and Target (1996) as "alien introjects." I believe Winnicott (1969) was referring to a similar phenomenon with his enigmatic phrase, "relating through identifications." I would say, following Winnicott, that our patients begin treatment relating to us (and themselves) "through" old identifications. Only as we are able to separate ourselves from our patients' identificatory systems—and, in so doing, help them begin to separate their true-self experience from old toxic identifications—can our patients begin to "use" their analysts as new objects (Winnicott, 1969; Newman et al., 1988). As I detail in Chapters 2 and 3 of this volume, it is the analyst's capacity to function as a "complex selfobject" that progressively *disables* the old toxic identifications, and *enables* needed transformations in the patient's experience of self and self-with-other.

I want to make clear, in concluding this brief review, that I am not sug-gesting that identification with the other's response to the self is the only basis on which our relationships to ourselves are constructed. For one, other kinds of identification are involved. A child may identify with the ways a parent treats themself or treats others (such as a sibling or the other parent). Beyond identification, another major determinant is a child's *accommo-dation* to the prevailing intersubjective contingencies (Brandchaft, 1994, 2010). A child may repress or disclaim affects, needs, or strivings because of the ways they are responded to (or not responded to) by needed others. The resulting relationship the child forms to these aspects of primary sub-jective experience is not an identification (although identificatory elements may be involved) but a defensive adaptation to the perceived requirements of the needed other (see also Bromberg, 2011). In addition, as the devel-opmental research literature has shown, when interactive regulation of a child's inner states is inadequate, the child tends to become excessively self-regulating (Tronick, 1989; Beebe and Lachmann, 1998)—a finding that supports Winnicott's (1962) concept of a "caretaker self." This kind of intrapsychic relationship is less an identification than a compensatory adaptation.

References

Beebe, B., & Lachmann, F.M. (1998). Co-constructing inner and relational processes: Self- and mutual regulation in infant research and adult treatment. *Psychoanalytic Psychology, 15*: 480–516.

Bollas, C. (1987). *The shadow of the object: Psychoanalysis of the unthought known.* New York, NY: Columbia University Press.

Brandchaft, B. (1994). To free the spirit from its cell. In R.D. Stolorow, G.E. Atwood, & B. Brandchaft, (Eds.), *The intersubjective perspective* (pp. 57–76). Northvale, NJ: Jason Aronson.

Brandchaft, B. (2010). Toward an emancipatory psychoanalysis. In B. Brandchaft, S. Doctors, & D. Sorter, *Toward an emancipatory psychoanalysis: Brandchaft's intersubjective vision* (pp. 9–27). New York, NY and London: Routledge.

Bromberg, P.M. (2011). *The shadow of the tsunami and the growth of the relational mind.* New York, NY and London: Routledge.

Fairbairn, W.R.D. (1952). *Psychoanalytic studies of the personality.* London: Tavistock.

Ferenczi, S. (1933/1980). Confusion of tongues between adults and the child. In M. Balint (Ed.), *Final contributions to the problems and methods of psychoanalysis* (pp. 156–167). London: Karnac.

Fonagy, P., & Target, M. (1996). Playing with reality: I. Theory of mind and the normal development of psychic reality. *International Journal of Psychoanalysis, 77*: 217–234.

Freud, S. (1917/1957). Mourning and melancholia. *Standard Edition, 14*: 239–258. London: Hogarth Press.

Freud, S. (1920/1955a). Beyond the pleasure principle. *Standard Edition, 18*: 1–64. London: Hogarth Press.

Freud, S. (1921/1955b). Group psychology and the analysis of the ego. *Standard Edition, 18*: 67–144. London: Hogarth Press.

Freud, S. (1923/1961). The ego and the id. *Standard Edition, 19*: 3–66. London: Hogarth Press.

Kohut, H. (1971). *The analysis of the self: A systematic approach to the psychoanalytic treatment of narcissistic personality disorders.* New York, NY: International Universities Press.

Kohut, H. (1977). *The restoration of the self.* New York, NY: International Universities Press.

Kohut, H. (1984). *How does analysis cure?* (A. Goldberg & P. Stepansky, Eds.). Chicago, IL: University of Chicago Press.

Laplanche, J., & Pontalis, J.-B. (1967/1973). *The language of psychoanalysis* (Donald Nicholson-Smith, Trans.). New York, NY: Norton.

Loewald, H. (1960/1980). On the therapeutic action of psychoanalysis. In *Papers on psychoanalysis* (pp. 221–256). New Haven, CT: Yale University Press.

Loewald, H. (1973/1980). On internalization. In *Papers on psychoanalysis* (pp. 6–86). New Haven, CT: Yale University Press.

Loewald, H. (1978/1980). Instinct theory, object relations and psychic structure formation. In *Papers on psychoanalysis* (pp. 207–218). New Haven, CT: Yale University Press.

Newman, K.M., Kligerman, C., and Terman, D.M. (1988). Countertransference: Its role in facilitating the use of the object. *Annual of Psychoanalysis, 16*: 251–276.

Ogden, T.H. (1994). *Subjects of analysis.* Northvale, NJ: Jason Aronson.

Sander, L. (1977). The regulation of exchange in the infant-caretaker system and some aspects of the context-content relationship. In M. Lewis & L. Rosenblum (Eds.), *Interaction, conversation, and the development of language* (pp. 133–156). New York, NY: Wiley.

Sander, L. (1985). Toward a logic of organization in psycho-biological development. In K. Klar & L. Siever (Eds.), *Biologic responses styles* (pp. 20–36). Washington, DC: American Psychiatric Press, .

Sander, L. (1995). Identity and the experience of specificity in aprocess of recognition: Commentary on Seligman and Shanok. *Psychoanalytic. Dialogues, 5*: 579–592.

Seligman, S. (1999). Integrating Kleinian theory and intersubjective infant research observing projective identification. *Psychoanalytic Dialogues, 9*: 129–159.

Stern, D.N. (1985), *The interpersonal world of the infant.* New York: Basic Books.

Stern, D.N., Sander, L.W., Nahum, J.P., Harrison, A.M., Lyons-Ruth, K., Morgan, A.C., Bruschweiler-Stern, N., & Tronick, E.Z. (1998). Non-interpretive mechanisms in psychoanalytic therapy: The "something more" than interpretation. *International Journal of Psycho-Analysis, 79*: 903–921.

Stolorow, R.D., & Atwood, G.E. (1992). *Contexts of being.* Hillsdale, NJ: The Analytic Press.

Tronick, E. (1989). Emotions and emotional communication in infants. *American Psychologist, 44*: 112–119.

Winnicott, D.W. (1962/1965). Ego integration in child development. In *The maturational processes and the facilitating environment* (pp. 56–63). London: Hogarth Press.

Winnicott, D.W. (1967/1971). Mirror-role of mother and family in child development. In *Playing and reality* (pp. 111–118). London: Tavistock Publications.

Winnicott, D.W. (1969/1971). The use of an object and relating through identifications. In *Playing and Reality* (pp. 86–94). London: Tavistock Publications.

Index

affects, capacity to experience and process 16
agency 11; airless worlds and 7, 15, 17, 24, 76–78; clinical material 28, 30, 81; self as agentic subject 16, 41, 58; separation-individuation and 17, 18; weakening/ disabling of the sense of i, 3, 5, 15, 24, 42
airless world syndrome i, 2–3, 6, 15, 19; factors affecting the severity and pervasiveness of 5–6; features 2–3, 6, 57, 72; and related psychoanalytic concepts ix–x, 6, 32, 33n1; treatment of 6–9; uniqueness of each case of 76; *see also* living in an airless world; *specific topics*
airless worlds viii; agency and 7, 15, 17, 24, 76–78; intersubjective airless worlds in couples 72, 73, 76–78; uniqueness of all 76; *see also* living in an airless world
airlessness 29, 75, 77, 78; varieties of 73–76
aloneness, sense of 16
alpha function 16
Alvarez, Anne 74
analytic adoption 93, 96–97, 109; clinical material 93; *see also* cases: Elizabeth; a crisis exposing the dark side of 103–105; mutual 92, 96, 97, 102–104, 111n2; nature of 109
analytic field 17
analytic frame 97; of potential warmth 48, 49; stretching the 92, 95–97
analytic reality principle 102
Anderson, James W. 94, 95
anorexia *see* cases: Mary
attachment conundrums, "impossible" 56, 60; *see also* cases: Philip

attachment theory 75, 117–118; pathological accommodation and 31
attachment to therapist, clinical material on 45, 98, 101, 102; *see also* attachment conundrums; cases: Philip
Atwood, George E. 40, 43, 97
autocatalysm, principle of 110
availability of therapist 96, 97, 100–101

Balint, Michael 100
Bass, Anthony 97
Beebe, Beatrice 117, 118
being: birth of a sense of 94; *see also* existential need
Benjamin, Jessica 20, 39, 77, 83; *see also* doer/done-to complementarity/dynamic
beta elements 16
Bion, Wilfred R. 16–17; negative capability 61; "without memory or desire" 9, 89
Bollas, Christopher 16, 59, 141, 142
bondage *see* identificatory bondage
Brandchaft, Bernard 31, 32; *see also* pathological accommodation
breathing, psychic ix, x, 5–7, 17, 18, 20, 37, 56; clinical material 83, 88
breathing together 44, 55, 69; clinical material 44, 49, 52, 55, 62, 63, 69, 70, 103, 135; selfobject relations and 7–9, 36, 44, 49, 52, 55, 135
Bromberg, Philip M. 17, 29–30; *see also* multiple-self-state theory; self-states

caretaker self (Winnicott) 143
cases: Clint 2, 42–44, 48, 52, 55; Elizabeth 31–32, 91–94, 98–110, 120; Jack and Ann 79–89; Kara (and Jim) 4–5; Kyle 118–123, 125–137; Lisa 3–5; Liz 24–30; Martha 36–37, 44–53, 55, 75; Martin

For Product Safety Concerns and Information please contact our EU
representative GPSR@taylorandfrancis.com
Taylor & Francis Verlag GmbH, Kaufingerstraße 24, 80331 München, Germany

www.ingramcontent.com/pod-product-compliance
Lightning Source LLC
Chambersburg PA
CBHW050611280326
41932CB00016B/2994

* 9 7 8 1 0 3 2 9 5 2 9 0 1 *